Giving

Wings

to
Children's
Dreams

For Paul

Best Wishes

Paul Houston

9-23-10

Making Our
Schools Worthy
of Our Children

A Joint Publication

CORWIN
A SAGE Company

AMERICAN ASSOCIATION
OF SCHOOL ADMINISTRATORS

For information:

Corwin
A SAGE Company
2455 Teller Road
Thousand Oaks,
 California 91320
(800) 233-9936
Fax: (800) 417-2466
www.corwin.com

SAGE India Pvt. Ltd.
B 1/I 1 Mohan Cooperative
 Industrial Area
Mathura Road,
 New Delhi 110 044
India

SAGE Ltd.
1 Oliver's Yard
55 City Road
London EC1Y 1SP
United Kingdom

SAGE Asia-Pacific Pte. Ltd.
33 Pekin Street #02-01
Far East Square
Singapore 048763

Printed in the United States of America

Library of Congress Cataloging-in-Publication Data

Houston, Paul D.
Giving wings to children's dreams : making our schools worthy of our children / Paul D. Houston; foreword by Terrence E. Deal. A Joint Publication With the American Association of School Administrators
    p. cm.
"A SAGE Company."
Includes bibliographical references and index.
ISBN 978-1-4129-8035-7 (pbk. : alk. paper)
    1. School improvement programs. I. Title.

LB2822.82.H68 2010
371.2'07—dc22   2010021135

This book is printed on acid-free paper.

10   11   12   13   14   10   9   8   7   6   5   4   3   2   1

Acquisitions Editor:	Arnis Burvikovs
Associate Editor:	Desirée Bartlett
Editorial Assistant:	Kimberly Greenberg
Production Editor:	Amy Schroller
Copy Editor:	Codi Bowman
Typesetter:	C&M Digitals (P) Ltd.
Proofreader:	Eleni-Maria Georgiou
Cover Designer:	Rose Storey

Contents

Foreword   v
Terrence E. Deal

About the Author   ix

Acknowledgments   xi

Introduction   1

1. My Wings   7
2. Teachers: Magicians and Conductors   15
3. Attitude = Altitude   23
4. Leaning Our Ladder Against the Right Wall   31
5. Crawling Out of the Box   39
6. How It Ought to Be   47
7. Getting Kids Ready for Democracy   55
8. Getting Kids Ready
   for School—Raising the Village   63
9. Getting Schools Ready for Kids   73
10. Getting the Words and Symbols Right   83
11. Horse Whispering: Harnessing
    Technology to Enhance Learning   91
12. The Brain Is a Terrible Thing to Waste   101
13. Creativity and the Arts:
    The Surrey, Not the Fringe   109
14. Authentic Accountability   119

15. Lead Is Not a Four-Letter Word   125
16. Bored of Education   133
17. Dealing With the Heart and Soul   141
18. A School Worthy of Our Children—A Fable   145

Study Guide   151
References   161

Foreword

There are several reasons I read whatever Paul Houston writes and trust his convictions: First, his early school experiences are very similar to mine. I hated my early years as a student. I, too, was labeled as dumb although my mind was always swirling with exciting ideas. I coped by inventing ways to cause trouble. Although typically successful in disrupting the classroom, when things didn't pan out, I became a runner. My secret hideout was the perfect place to read what interested me and think great thoughts. Later on, occasional bursts of "brilliance" earned me the label of "under-achiever." Only the threats of a stint with the California Youth Authority or the loss of a football scholarship made me buckle down and become a late blooming "gifted" scholar. Like Paul, I know what it's like to walk in the shoes of a variety of student roles. I also feel beholden to Mrs. Krantz, Mr. Dezutti, Walter Meyers, and other teachers who saw something in me that I couldn't see at the time.

Second, Paul's rich background as a teacher, principal, super-intendent, and experience at policy levels equip him to view education from a number of unique perspectives. As a consequence, he is able to see the possibilities and pitfalls of educational reform from classroom to senate cloakroom. He recognizes that, for a long time, the lack of communication across levels has hampered efforts to improve schools. The result is a carousel of reforms that never stick. They fail but pop up relabeled only to fall short again. Paul understands that we are climbing a ladder propped against a rational wall of standards, testing, and pay for performance, which is getting us nowhere.

Third, unlike most educational scholars and policy analysts, Paul is able to peep beneath the veneer of rationality to appre-hend the more ephemeral underbelly of schools as organizations.

The dominant view holds that schools exist to impart existing knowledge rather than cultivate students' imaginations as a source of new ideas. This has hampered America's ability to innovate, once the country's competitive advantage in the global economy. Lack of imagination was also cited by a National Commission as a contributing cause of our failure to ward off the terrorist attack on the World Trade Center: "We believe the 9/11 attack revealed four kinds of failures: imagination, policy, capabilities, and management" (National Commission on Terrorist Attacks upon the United States, 2004, p. 343).

Information Versus Imagination

Albert Einstein once observed, "The gift of fantasy has meant more to me than my talent for absorbing positive knowledge." Positive knowledge is now readily available at our fingertips. At times, staying abreast of information seems overwhelming. Some describe the flow as drinking from a fire hose. Conversely, fantasies, or dreams, take us below or behind information to ferret out what it means. Students today are asked to master the "what" without going the next steps of exploring the "what if" or the "why not." Both questions require imagination, fantasy, or a sense of playfulness. Such questions take us to a wellspring of innovation. Thomas Edison put it bluntly: "To innovate, all you need is a good imagination and a pile of junk." Fanciful minds will find something of value in apparent disorder or seeming error. Both Ivory soap and Scotch tape were conceived by creative people who saw promise in unfortunate mistakes.

In the business world, innovation is a top priority. Apple's original slogan "Think Different," AT&T's "Rethink Possible," and GE's current slogan "Innovation at Work" are prime examples. Imagine today's students, who are used to acquiring or mastering information, entering the world of work and being asked to dream up new practices or products. The brute fact is that schools are not preparing students for the challenges they will intimately confront. To equip students to tackle present and future demands, we need to balance rigor and vigor, conformity and divergence, work and playfulness, and correct answers and provocative questions. Paul presents a blueprint for how that might be done.

Blueprint for the Future

Swirling around the question of how to improve education is a question of its ultimate purpose. Paul takes us back in history to examine the evolution of education's mission over the decades. It began with the goal of religious training and preparing students to become productive citizens. As quoted in *Education Week*, Larry Cuban (2001) summarizes the following:

> Tax supported schools in the United States were not established one hundred and fifty years ago to ensure jobs for graduates or to replace family or church. They were established to make sure children would grow into literate adults that respect authority and make reasoned judgments, accept differences of opinion, and fulfill their civic duty to participate in the political and social life of their communicates. (Harris, P. & Smith, B., 2010, May 12).

When factories replaced farms, the purpose evolved to developing skills and, ultimately, began to measure how well schools were doing. We are now at a time when acquiring knowledge and developing tests to measure progress dominate the educational agenda and eclipse other important purposes. The hands and heads of students receive ample attention as long as rational motives are considered. Their imaginations, hearts, and souls are ignored.

Paul's blueprint presumes that the primary purposes of education is to develop students who know themselves, have character, are able to think divergently, and will ultimately be able to assume their place in a fast-paced, constantly changing society. Rather than begin the search for goals at the policy levels, he starts with the interests of students. The job of a teacher is to capture these interests and tailor them into productive activities that help students grow and achieve worthy aims with enthusiasm and pluck. Innovation rather than recitation and reiteration predominate. He provides examples of schools in the United States and abroad that have been able to put these purposes into practice. Every school district in this country should take this blueprint seriously.

The chief problem with schools today is not producing scores on standardized tests; it is reviving the soul and spirit necessary to accomplish one of the important tasks a society can undertake.

If we would change education's mantra from "every child a test score" to "every child a promise," we would be well along the road to improvement. Paul presents a way this sacrosanct undertaking can be realized. Teachers are the catalyst for the dreams and the wind beneath students' wings. Read on. Enjoy the ideas and put them to work.

Terrence E. Deal

About the Author

 **Paul D. Houston** currently serves as president of the Center for Empowered Leadership and executive director emeritus of the American Association of School Administrators (AASA). Previously, Houston served more than 14 years as its executive director. Prior to AASA, Houston served as superintendent of three very different school districts: Princeton, New Jersey; Tucson, Arizona; and Riverside, California. Houston has also served as an assistant superintendent in Birmingham, Alabama; as a principal in Summit, New Jersey; and as teacher and principal in Chapel Hill, North Carolina.

Houston holds degrees from the Ohio State University, the University of North Carolina, and Harvard University. Houston has received numerous honors including an honorary doctorate from Duquesne University, the Richard R. Green award for leadership in urban education from the Council of Great City Schools, the Courageous Leadership award from the Hope Foundation, and the Outstanding Educator award from the Horace Mann League. In 2008, he received the prestigious American Education award from AASA. In 2009, he received the Learning and Liberty award from the National School Public Relations Association.

Houston's extensive writing includes nearly 300 articles in various professional magazines and journals. He has coauthored three books, *Exploding the Myths* (1993), *The Board-Savvy Superintendent* (2003), and *The Spiritual Dimension of Leadership* (2006). He has also authored three collections of essays, *Articles of Faith and Hope for Public Education* (1996), *Outlook and Perspectives on American Education* (2003), and *No Challenge Left Behind* (2008).

He is also coeditor for a series of books from Corwin Press on the soul of educational leadership. These include *Engaging Every Learner* (2007), *Out of the Box Leadership* (2007), *Sustaining Professional Learning Communities* (2008), *Spirituality in Educational Leadership* (2008), *Leaders as Communicators and Diplomats* (2009), *Building Sustainable Leadership Capacity* (2009), *Data Enhanced Leadership* (2010), and *Leadership for Community and Family Involvement* (2010).

Houston has established himself as a leading spokesperson for American public education through his extensive U.S. and international speaking engagements and his media interviews.

Acknowledgments

Writing is, at its core, a lonely exercise. You sit at the computer for hours, all alone, thinking of what is important to you and what you hope your reader will get from the words you share. But the well that you draw from has been filled by others. I am grateful for all those teachers, administrators, board members, and professors who have filled my well. I am especially thankful for those teachers I mention in the book: Mrs. Spurlock, Mrs. Crum, Miss Reynolds, Mr. Ball, and Mrs. Sang because without you, I would not have learned to read and embrace the larger world, would not have thought of being a writer, would not have developed a sense of myself and the world I am responsible for in my small way, and I certainly would have never dared to dream the dreams that propelled me forward.

I have to thank all those staff who were subjected to my out-of-the-box leadership at the various schools and systems I led: Lincoln and Beekman Terrace Elementary Schools, Birmingham Public Schools, Princeton Regional School District, Tucson Unified School District, and the Riverside Unified School District. Further, I had the gift of serving the Superintendents of America for more than 14 years as the executive director of the American Association of School Administrators where I learned much more than I taught, and the honor of serving them still humbles me. I have been buoyed by family, friends, and those who loved me—most especially, my children who served as fodder for my stories and inspirations for what is possible and Jesse Rodriquez who offered a warm smile and a glass of cool wine just when it was most needed. And I want to thank Sandy Chapman whose clarity took me home. In fact, Sandy pushed me to start this book, and she pushed me to finish it. Still having the remnants of a slow learner inside of me, it was great to receive her encouragement.

Of course, I appreciate the good folks at Corwin/Sage Publishing who helped make sense of the writing and had the good sense (in my humble opinion) to see the need for this book. And last but certainly not least, I am grateful for you, dear reader, because the fact that you hold this book in your hands tells me that you wish for something better for our children and that wish can become a dream, and that dream can change the world.

Publisher's Acknowledgments

Corwin gratefully acknowledges the contributions of the following reviewers:

Seidah Ashshaheed
Principal
King George Middle School
King George, VA

Franklin CampbellJones,
Vice President
CampbellJones & Associates
Capeville, VA

Kathleen Cushman
Author, *Fires in the Mind: What Kids Can Tell Us About Motivation and Mastery*
Cofounder, What Kids Can Do (www.WKCD.org)
New York, NY

Sheila Gragg
Assistant Director of Academics
Ashbury College
Ottawa, Ontario, Canada

Kristopher R. Kwiatek
Assistant Principal
Seoul American Elementary School
Department of Defense Dependant Schools
Seoul, Korea

Roberto A. Pamas,
Principal
O.W. Holmes Middle School
Falls Church, VA

William Sommers,
Director of Learning Alternatives
Spring Lake Park Schools
Spring Lake Park, MN

Introduction

I have worked as an educator for more than 40 years. Although much has changed over that time, there have been a few constants. One is that I have found that most of the criticism leveled at schools has been misdirected and off the point. The second constant is that most of the people working in education are not shiftless, lazy unionists with no interest in children. They are dedicated to the task of "touching the future" as Christa McAuliffe put it. The third constant is that education, at its core, is not complicated. It is about the relationships between the people and about the processes that must be undertaken to connect them. It is, in essence, an organic process. It is mostly about uplifting and challenging people in meaningful ways.

I come to this book with strong biases borne out of my experience as a student and as a teacher, principal, superintendent, and national education association executive. I grew up in a place called Davis Creek, West Virginia. My trajectory took me to a number of schools, two major public universities, and ultimately, to the ivy covered rarefied atmosphere of Harvard University. I taught in a blue-collar section of Durham, North Carolina, and the newly integrated Chapel Hill public schools. I was a principal in Chapel Hill and later in the upper-middle-class suburb of Summit, New Jersey. I was an assistant superintendent in Birmingham, Alabama, during a time of great turmoil in the south and superintendent of schools in three very distinctly different school districts. I spent nine years in the Princeton Regional Schools in Princeton, New Jersey, one of the most highly educated communities in the United States, more than five years in the urbanized southwest in Tucson, Arizona, and three years in Riverside, California, an edge city on the edge of the country. I followed this up with more than 14 years as executive director of

1

the American Association of School Administrators. Each of these experiences colored and expanded my understanding of the good, bad, and ugly of American education.

I came away from all this with a simple philosophy. Schools are about creating and nurturing dreams, and this is best done through meaningful, engaging work. I believe that we have to view education as *fundamental* not merely *instrumental*. In other words, it isn't about preparation for life or work—it *is* life and work—right here, right now. It isn't something you "invoke" and pour into children. It is something you "evoke" and draw from them. One of the biggest problems we have in education today is that we are trying to force learning into children, and when you force something, you break it. There are basic truths about what motivates and inspires people and these must be embedded in the educational process. The American education system has great diversity and inequities built into it, but at its core, it is simply about acting more as an elevator than a bulldozer. It is about raising people up, not flattening them out.

The current discussions about education are either misdirected or mistaken, and this has been true for at least the last 50 years. The names change, the issues morph, the policies are modified, but basically, education is affected by four *dirty Ds*, as I call them.

The first is *distraction*. We are constantly being distracted from focusing on the real problems of education by issues that are raised by political and corporate leaders who neither understand education nor really seem to care that much about it. Although education is fundamental to a healthy society, it is down on the list of issues that political people consider, and when they bring it up, it is usually to promote an idea or pet project that won't really change things. For business leaders, education is important until it comes time to tax themselves to support it. For example, we have seen a major emphasis on accountability in the last few years, as defined by measuring the outcomes of multiple-choice tests. Success in life isn't about filling in a bubble on an answer sheet, and yet that has become the standard because it has been forced onto education by elected officials. The Elementary and Secondary Education Act that first passed in the 1960s to assist poor students has morphed into the No Child Left Behind (NCLB) law that puts a premium on test results for all children. This is distracting educators from acting on the deeper things we should be giving children.

For more than 20 years, many have proposed giving vouchers to parents so they can choose their children's schools. The idea is that competition is good and will force improved education. I must observe this is the model used by Wall Street and the big banks. How has that worked for us? A paucity of evidence shows when family income is held as a constant, choice schools perform better than public schools; yet politicians and neoconservative pundits continue to push vouchers. They are simply promoting distraction. The great irony here is that the schools held up as exemplars of excellence—private schools—are not required to meet the imposed, coercive policies aimed at public schools and are allowed to choose their students, something public schools cannot and should not do. It is easy to win a competition if you get to pick all your players and play by your rules.

The second dirty D is *distortion*. If you can't distract the public and educators from working on the right issues, then distort the reality of the current situation. This is most clearly seen in media stories about education where the most extreme issues and situations are reported without context or comment. When I was superintendent in Tucson, we had an outbreak of hepatitis, and all headlines and evening news shows screamed about "Hepatitis in the Tucson Unified Schools." Well, there were several cases in one school, but it was found that the children had contracted the disease in their neighborhood from tainted water. It had nothing to do with the school. Despite being notified of this, the media continued to use the schools headline for days. I have always found some gallows humor in the headlines around murders. If a body was found anywhere, it was usually described as "near, such and such school," as if the school had something to do with the death. The next time a serial killer is caught, check and see if there isn't something mentioned about which schools they attended—never mind the churches or boy scout troop they may have belonged to. In many cases, the distortion comes merely by placing the wrong focus on the story. In others, it is from misunderstanding the issue. Newspapers love to rank schools by their test scores. If they ranked the communities by family income, it would have an eerie overlap with the school list. Might one affect the other? We'll never know from the reporting that goes on.

The third D is *disrespect*. This hit home for me after having the opportunity to visit other nations and to look at their schools.

Most were not nearly as good as those found in the United States, yet there was a pride in the schools we rarely see here and a respect for educators that simply does not exist in America. On my visit to Singapore, I found that the government totally underwrites the cost of teacher training, and then it pays the teachers more than doctors, lawyers, and engineers because of the recognition that you wouldn't have these professions without teachers. I visited muddy villages along the Amazon where the school was the nicest hut in the village. Around the world, I found other countries had greater respect for educators and for the educational process than we find here. I saw children walking miles in the remote reaches of the Masai Mora in Kenya, so they could go to school because getting an education was the most important thing they could do. In America, we are fond of reciting, "Those who can do, and those who can't, teach." We see the teachers attacked as moneygrubbing hacks when they simply would like to maintain a modicum of self-respect. Education must be valued by the student and family, but it must also be valued by the society that supports it.

The fourth and perhaps most powerful dirty D is *disadvantage*. This has been written about eloquently by such people as my friend Jonathan Kozol, in such books as *Savage Inequalities* and *Amazing Grace* (1991, 1995). The first time I met Jonathan, I teased him that I had lived his *Savage Inequalities* book, from my upbringing in rural West Virginia, to my stint in affluent Summit and Princeton to my time in Tucson, which was spending a fraction on students compared to what I saw in Princeton. Today, we are seeing a push for national standards so that we can be assured that all our children will be competitive in the growingly complex global economy. That is fine; will we also see a national standard for supporting education? I doubt it. During the years of NCLB, I was in Washington, the epicenter of policymaking. And do you know what? It was considered bad form to mention poverty as an intervening variable for student achievement. Well, talking about student achievement without talking about the effects of poverty is like NASA talking about going to the moon but failing to consider gravity as an intervening variable. Poverty, like gravity, can be overcome. But going to the moon took a big rocket and a lot of fuel. And yet we expect to deliver education on the cheap. We have pundits, including a couple of former secretaries of education, who opine that money doesn't matter. The only people I have ever heard say that are people who already have money. Go into the South Bronx or the Navajo Reservation or a barrio in East Los Angeles and try that out. Yes, money is not sufficient to delivering good education, but it is necessary, and to ignore that reality is the worst level of distortion, distraction, and disrespect.

But I don't want to let the education community off totally. Educators continue to cling to outmoded ways of teaching and educating. We add to the inequality when we have contracts that put the weakest teachers in the schools where the hardest to educate attend. We settle for mediocrity when we could create excellence, and we give children experiences that are totally disconnected from what interests them, and we keep parents and communities at arm's length when we need to embrace them. We continue to ignore the fact that education is really about people's hearts as much as it is about their minds. It is about their possibilities as much as it is about their performance.

Education has to be oriented toward creating success in students. It has to focus on the assets they bring with them so they can be built on. We can transform our schools in America. But the most important transformation has to come from our internal transformation of understanding what education is really about. It is about giving wings to children's dreams and that is what I have tried to capture in this book.

My daughter Lisa and her husband Jason gave me two wonderful grandchildren who are really what this book is all about. And Sandy has brought her granddaughter Jade into my world to round things out. So for Will and Lucy Harding and Jade Belden my wish is that all your dreams have wings and that we can make our schools and our world worthy of you.

CHAPTER ONE

My Wings

I can't go back to yesterday because I was a different person then.

—Lewis Carroll

I grew up in rural West Virginia, the son of a Methodist Minister. When I was five, we moved to Davis Creek, a very small community a few miles outside of Huntington. There was no kindergarten in those days, so a year later, I entered first grade in the little school down the road from my house with great expectations but no preparation. I was 1 of 50 students in the classroom, and I proceeded to get lost in the herd. Further, I lived through my imagination and had a tendency to daydream. Consequently, I failed to learn how to read and even had problems with the alphabet.

Today, there is a lot of controversy about *social promotion,* and many states and systems have moved away from it. I must confess; I am very thankful that it was around when I was young, or I would be the oldest first grader in America today. The controversy over social promotion is typical of the way education policy is made. Politicians decide that something doesn't make sense, and they pass policies to do away with it. Never mind that research has been pretty consistent that students tend to do worse when repeating a grade than they do if passed forward with inadequate skills. Neither is a great option, but the one that works best tends to be the counterintuitive one. Most educators understand this;

most politicians do not. It highlights the perils of amateurs making professional decisions. Fortunately for me, in those days, the politicians hadn't yet taken over, so I moved on, without a lot of skills but with my imagination intact.

Because of overcrowding, I was moved on to second grade the next year and fared no better there. I continued to enjoy the dreams and visions inside my head, but outside, things were becoming more of a nightmare. I was in a fog most of the time and had no idea what was going on. School was a mystery to me, and it wasn't much fun. I felt stupid most of the time and thought there had to be a better place than school to spend my time. Once again, they moved me on, so I went to third grade not knowing how to read and thinking school was a complete waste of my time.

I entered third grade with Mrs. Spurlock, who was a very imposing woman. Through my eight-year-old eyes, she seemed to be about eight-feet tall and weighed about 3,000 pounds. She was stern and a little scary. And she discovered two things about me. First, she realized I couldn't read a bit. I had no idea if Spot was running or eating the rug. She also saw that my mind wandered. In today's world, they may say I had attention deficit disorder, but in those days, they just said, "His mind wanders." She set about trying to rid me of both problems.

For my mind wandering, she had a very simple pedagogical technique. She seated me in front of the class, and when she noticed my mind wandering, she applied the end of her yardstick to the top of my head, which refocused my attention and opened my mind to new learning vistas. Her approach to my reading deficit was just as direct and simple. She sat with me to start the process and then piled stacks of books in my arms each afternoon with the expectation I would read them at home and could talk about them the next day. Her techniques and, more important, her expectations let me leave her room at the end of the year a very avid reader. I started reading books about the frontier and about faraway lands. Mrs. Spurlock opened the world to me, and for that, I will always love her.

The rest of my elementary career consisted of struggling to make it through the day and the year. My life outside the classroom was filled with interesting things to do and see. I spent a lot of time down by the creek looking for crayfish. I made up games with my friends. I had a fascination with television to the point that I created a studio in my house and put on my own programs. I had to give up my studio during my third-grade year because we finally got indoor plumbing, and my studio became a bathroom. I will leave to your imagination what sort of metaphor that creates for current television programming. I made up plays with my friends and put them on for the neighborhood. But in the classroom, I was still a "day late and a dollar short," as my mother put it.

When I was in fourth grade, we moved several times, and I always seemed to miss long division. I stumbled and fumbled my way through each year and received my first label—*slow learner.* Although I had this wonderfully rich world inside my head, it didn't seem to translate to my classrooms. I was known as a storyteller, but that didn't gain me any points either. The teachers thought that I daydreamed too much and wondered about my veracity, as sometimes my stories were quite vivid and clearly made up. Also, when discussions were held I would come up with answers that made a lot of sense to me but were way outside the scope of the discussion. The teachers and my fellow classmates would look at me as if I were one of those Martians from some UFO we were hearing about in the news. Further, I would offer my unique insights that were instantly ignored because they were so divergent only to hear a classmate come up with a similar insight 15 minutes later that was praised by the teacher. That was my first realization that lateral, divergent thinking wasn't welcome in most classrooms of the day. Actually, as a child, my biggest insight was that I must be really, really dumb. Everyone else seemed to be on the same page, and I couldn't even find the book.

As I moved into junior high school, I started doing pretty well on the achievement tests but was still struggling in the classroom, so I got my second label—*underachiever.* The teachers felt I could do the work but I just wouldn't. I don't remember it that way at all. I was doing the best I could to fit my round self into their square classrooms. I wasn't holding back. The whole thing just didn't make much sense to me, and the life I had outside the school was a lot more interesting than the one I had inside. My friends and I would play very elaborate board games, we would create very imaginative games in the woods near our homes, we continued to create plays and performances for the neighborhood, and I continued to read voraciously the books that interested me. None of this had much to do with my schooling. I barely got out of junior high school making straight *D* minuses in ninth-grade English. You had to pass that class to be promoted, and I barely cleared that bar.

As I moved into high school, all my tumblers fell into place. Suddenly, school became easy for me. My grades shot up, the work seemed easier, and I got yet another label—*gifted*. Looking back, I realize that my learning style is very right-brained, and I had been living in a left-brained world. American schools and most others I have visited around the world are very Procrustean in design. Procrustes was a character from Greek mythology who was an innkeeper. However, he had only one bed in his inn, so when a visitor came, he would measure the guest. If they were too long for the bed, he chopped off their legs. If they were too short, he had a rack he would put them on to stretch them to the right size. I had spent the first nine years of my school life being sliced and diced or pulled and stretched to fit the educational model available instead of the model building off my gifts and talents. High school wasn't easier because they had suddenly personalized my education; it was easier because I had finally learned to play the game.

One day in Mrs. Crum's 10th-grade English class, she came up to me and asked me a question I continue to grapple with to this day. She asked, "Have you ever thought about being a writer?" Now, I was the guy who had barely escaped ninth-grade English. What kind of question was that? But if she saw something in me that I hadn't seen in myself, maybe I should take a look. Now, six books and hundreds of articles later, I guess I am a writer. And much of the credit goes to Mrs. Crum for planting that seed.

Teachers and administrators plant seeds every day in children. Sometimes they are seeds of possibility and hope like the one Mrs. Crum planted in me. But far too often, they are seeds of doubt and despair. The question of "How can I?" is a much more empowering question than the one of "What if I can't?" Teachers need to be in the empowerment business. I was lucky that I had a Mrs. Crum to ask the right question at the right time. It empowered me. It opened up a new world to me.

I had three other teachers in high school that did the same. Miss Reynolds my high school drama teacher took a shy, doubting boy under her wing and gave him the confidence to go on stage and ham it up. I have often wondered what she would think of me today, standing in front of thousands of people giving a motivational speech or appearing on live national television. I suspect she would recognize the seeds of possibility she had planted in me. She also gave me permission to look inside myself, to examine my self-doubts and my sensitivities, to know that is part of our human passage, and to be courageous enough to be open about them. Most of us spend the majority of our lives hiding ourselves from others. To become powerful you have to be willing to see and acknowledge your weaknesses. It is only in risking your vulnerability that you can become powerful. Miss Reynolds taught me how to do that.

Mr. Ball was my social studies teacher. He took a deadly topic and made it live for all of us. He talked about historical figures as if he knew them. He brought history to life for us and let us understand that social science isn't just about learning people, events, and dates. It is about understanding the human condition. This was aided by the fact that he knew every cliché and aphorism known to man and sprinkled them into his lectures and discussions. Now, the reason a cliché is an overused expression is that is true. There is wisdom in it. And Mr. Ball's words stuck with me. To this day, I hear his voice in my head. If I am having a bad day, I hear Mr. Ball saying, "This too shall pass." And he's right. It does. Mr. Ball wasn't teaching social studies nearly as much as he was teaching resilience. He taught us how to face life with all its problems with resolve and to know that everything that was happening to us had happened a million times to others in the past.

I also remember Mr. Ball coming to our 20th graduation reunion. He got up in front of us and reminded us of our class motto, "Our hopes are high; success is in God's hands." He then proceeded to tell us that it was about the dumbest motto any class had ever picked because if we had not been successful it wasn't God's fault; it was ours. And as he looked at us, he said he didn't think we had made as much of ourselves as we should, and he would be at the next reunion to check us out. And sure enough, he was! Education is something that sticks with you—usually figuratively like Mr. Ball's aphorisms but sometimes literally like his continued interest in our success. Education is also about helping you see that personal responsibility is paramount. Success isn't up to someone else. It is up to each of us. I learned a little about that from Mr. Ball.

Mrs. Sang was my Latin teacher and a good friend and major pain in my life. She was constantly making me try harder and do better. First, Latin wasn't the most electrifying of subjects. But if I wanted to take a major translation exercise and turn it into a musical comedy, she let me. She understood that creativity needed to be nourished and that the outcome was learning the bigger lessons of life and not the smaller ones required for a grade.

She asked me one day if I was going to college. I told her, "No. I don't think I am college material." You see, even though at that point I carried the label of gifted, it often is the early labels and the more negative ones that are the most powerful. I may have been gifted to the school, but in my heart and soul, I was still a slow learner. Mrs. Sang begged to differ, and we had a number of heated discussions around my going to college. At the end of the day, she won. I was one of a handful of my class that went on to college.

A number of years later, I was the superintendent of schools for the Princeton, New Jersey, school district. I was back in my hometown in West Virginia visiting my parents, and I went down to the old high school. I ran into Mrs. Sang, still teaching in the same classroom, now in the twilight of her career. She was teaching French because they had dropped Latin from the curriculum. I ran into her during a passing period, and we started catching up. When the bell rang, she pulled me into her classroom, sat me in front of the class, and started asking questions, as she had when I was a student. Only this time they were about me.

"Did you go to college?"
"Yes, I did."
"Where?"
"The Ohio State University"
"Did you get a master's degree?"
"Yes I did."
"Where?"
"The University of North Carolina."
"Do you have a doctor's degree?"
"Yes I do."
"Where did you get that?"
"Harvard University."

And then she proceeded to ask me about my work experience. So I shared my teaching career, my time as a principal and as an assistant superintendent, and then about my time in my first superintendency. Then she asked me about my travels. After about 15 minutes of this Socratic dialogue, she got to the money question.

"Where did you go to high school?"
"Well, I went right here."

And at that point, the class erupted.

"No way!"
"No he didn't!"
"Not possible!"

She signaled for quiet.

"Why would you say that? Didn't he just tell you he did go here?"

One of the students gave her the answer she was expecting.

"Because people who have done what he has done don't go to this high school."

She knew that was the attitude. She was just using me as an advanced audiovisual technique to teach those young people that they didn't have to limit themselves or their dreams to the heights of the hills that surrounded that rural West Virginia high school.

Mrs. Sang understood the soft bigotry of low expectations long before they were articulated by national politicians. She understood that education has one basic mission—to give wings to children's dreams.

I tell my story not because it is unique but because it is so typical. Millions of children go to class everyday in America. Far too often, it is in classrooms that are still too Procrustean in their design, where a one-size-fits-all curriculum meets an incredibly diverse and unique set of children. But millions also go to class with teachers who despite state and federal mandates are still trying to plant seeds of possibility in their children; to give them the world; to help them understand that if they take responsibility, they can become something more than they think. And there are teachers trying to give wings to their dreams. Trying to make these teachers and these classrooms more than heroic exceptions is the challenge of education reform, and that is what this book is all about.

CHAPTER TWO

Teachers

Magicians and Conductors

I touch the future; I teach.

—Christa McAuliffe

Teachers are at the center of the educational process. From the days of Socrates, when he sat on a log with his student, the teacher and student are what education is about. All of us remember the teachers we had who made a difference like Mrs. Sang or Mrs. Spurlock, but we also remember those who made our lives difficult through their indifference. It is interesting that it is not the hard teachers we remember with disdain—it is the ones who didn't care. When you strip away all the degrees and the training of teachers, when you take away union membership or alternative certification, it all comes down to the reality that those teachers who care about each child are the ones who succeed. Pedagogical techniques and colleges attended don't matter—caring does.

My first year as an administrator, I had Mrs. Dunn (name changed to protect the innocent) who was one of my special education teachers. Let me offer a disclaimer here that her techniques and her language are not something I suggest others emulate. I would suggest that we could all learn from the essence of who she was and what she did for children. Mrs. Dunn was an African American lady of indeterminate age and incalculable weight. And all the kids in the school were scared to death of her. Truth be told, so were the teachers. The prior year, I had a student, Melvin, who was the toughest and scariest kid in school. One day, on his return from the bathroom, he rushed into the class with terror etched on his face.

"What's the matter Melvin?" I asked.

"I was going past Mrs. Dunn's class, and I kind of peeked in, and she jumped up and ran at me and told me if I didn't get my face out of her door, she was going to rip off my arm and beat me to death with it."

Now, the fact that Mrs. Dunn could not just make such an outrageous threat but could sell it to the toughest kid in school speaks volumes for her credibility.

When I took over as building principal, as a callow 25-year-old with little teaching experience, one of my biggest worries was Mrs. Dunn. How could I get her to tone it down? What would I do if she tried to rip my arm off and beat me to death with it? What I found was that even though all the other kids in the school were afraid of her—the children in her class loved her.

That year, she had been sent a girl who was thrown out of all her previous schools. She had been arrested for breaking into cars. She was 10 years old, mildly mentally handicapped, severely emotionally disturbed, and on the fast track to prison. And I never heard a peep from her all year. In fact, when I visited the classroom (at Mrs. Dunn's invitation of course because I wanted to keep both my arms), I noticed the girl was always hard at work, and her interactions with her classmates, Mrs. Dunn, or even me were sweet and pleasant. I asked Mrs. Dunn one day how she had transformed that scary girl into a model student. She told me it wasn't hard. She understood the girl's environment. She was being raised by an abusive father, with no mother at home, and no hope. She was acting out to get some kind of attention.

Mrs. Dunn just said, "She knows I love her and will take care of her. If she's hungry, I feed her. If she needs money, I give it to her. And if she needs a hug, she gets it. She knows I love her and will do anything for her. But she also knows that if she steps out of line, I'll get her good."

Mrs. Dunn had a BA from a second-rate college. She wasn't particularly intellectually smart, but she was brilliant enough to know what kids needed, and she gave it to them. For most of her kids, that meant structure. Mrs. Dunn told me a story of when she had gone into teaching after her children had entered school. The school assigned her a class that had already driven three teachers out, and it was only January. Sure enough, on her first day, the kids were terrible. She said she went home and cried and told her husband she wasn't going back. But she did.

The next morning she told the kids, in her sweetest voice, "You know, yesterday, you children were so bad to Mrs. Dunn that I went home and told my husband I wasn't coming back. But you know. I need this job, so here I am. And the first one who gives me a hard time, his a%# is going out the door. And the next one, well her a%# is going out the window." She told me, "Now I know I'm not supposed to talk that way, but that is what they understand. I had to get their attention before I could teach them. And they were a great class the rest of the year."

Her kids, even though they were castoffs from the regular school program, achieved much better than many of the kids in the regular classes. She provided structure for their unstructured lives, she set high expectations for them, and she gave them love and support. And she worked them hard. She used to say, "Just because these kids are in special education doesn't mean they can't work."

Over the years, I had a chance to see and work with other great teachers. They had many different kinds of backgrounds, skills, and philosophies. But they all had one thing in common. They took pride in what they did, and they cared deeply about the kids they worked with.

I worked with other teachers, some of whom were brilliant and had outstanding academic credentials. But they weren't happy in their work. The kids drove them crazy, and they desperately wanted to be somewhere else. And they just weren't very good teachers. They spent most of their time in the teacher's lounge complaining about their classes and talking about how they would like to be doing something else. And they should.

I am not saying any of this to disparage teachers, teacher education, credentialing, and the like. I have nothing against teacher unions, which sometimes support bad teachers. That is why teachers pay their dues. These are all perhaps necessary—they just don't make for better teaching. Just as students need to be motivated, so do teachers. And the core of that motivation has to be caring (may I suggest love) for children.

After that, things begin to vary. I have seen great teachers who are a bit formal in their relationships with students but who have extremely high expectations and who support the students in meeting them. I have seen others, who despite the warning of not touching children, touch them and hug them at every opportunity.

Some of the best I have ever seen have developed their own methods and even, to some extent, their own curriculum. When my oldest daughter, Lisa, entered Mrs. Pat Van Ness's kindergarten class in Princeton, New Jersey, she was already a capable reader. I had been told Mrs. Van Ness was the best kindergarten teacher in the district. But after a few weeks, I wasn't so sure. The work Lisa was bringing home clearly indicated that Mrs. Van Ness didn't seem to know that Lisa could already read. I went to see her and to express my concern. She told me that she knew Lisa could read, but as a self-taught reader, she didn't have the skills to become a great reader. She asked me to give her until the winter break to prove her methods.

A few days after Christmas, we were sitting around the kitchen table. Lisa picked up the New York Times that I had been reading and started reading the front page—perfectly. I asked her what the story was about and she understood it. She wasn't just sounding out the words. She had word-attack skills and comprehension. Mrs. Van Ness had worked her magic. I found out that she didn't really follow the district curriculum for kindergarten. She had her own techniques and materials. And every year, every child who went through her class left as accomplished readers and motivated students. Now, as superintendent, I could have pulled her back and forced her to follow the district curriculum. But all I would have accomplished would have been to take a magically gifted and motivated teacher and turn her into an unhappy mediocre one.

As the nation has pushed hard in the direction of accountability and that accountability has been defined as an external imposition of rewards and punishments, we have seen an exodus of teachers from schools all across the country. And it hasn't been the mediocre teachers—it has been the good ones. We can't afford to lose these people, and we need to look at what we are doing to them.

Teaching is an act of creation and conscience. If those things are removed from the equation, the ones who aren't bothered by their loss are the ones already operating without them, and they are not the teachers who should be working with children. Those who depend on themselves for bringing forth the best in students are handicapped by external pressures and methods. You would never take a racehorse and hitch it to a plow. We shouldn't be taking great teachers and treating them like we treat the mediocre ones. The problem of a one-size-fits-all approach is that it isn't just bad for children—it is devastating to good teachers.

Lisa, that little five-year-old who reaped the magic of Pat Van Ness, is now in her mid-thirties and teaching herself. She recently won the outstanding teacher award in the private school where she teaches. She teaches in a private school because, although she was a Magna Cum Laude and Phi Beta Kappa graduate of an Ivy League school, she lacks the teaching credentials to work in a public school. Now, not every honors graduate from an Ivy League school should be in a classroom (Teach for America notwithstanding). It takes more than intellectual firepower to be a good teacher. But in Lisa's case, she couples her intellectual ability with a deep love of her students.

I have gotten to watch her in action. She teaches drama, and her plays involve a large percentage of the entire student body. If she can't find a play that works for her kids, she finds original material and adapts it for the stage. She chooses really hard work for the kids and doesn't say much about it. She just lets them know what her expectations are. And she really cares about them. She is invested in their total lives and intervenes if she sees them going off track in other classes. And when they graduate, she keeps up with them. They come back and some even help as volunteers. Teaching for Lisa is a 24/7 proposition, and the only times she gets frustrated about the work is when an administrator interferes. Left to her devices and with a little support, she works magic.

Obviously, with more than two million teachers in America, not everyone will be a magician. But you can't create magicians by dictating the tricks they need to perform. And you can't make them caring mentors by treating them in an uncaring fashion.

Another great teacher that I was able to observe was Bill Trego, the choir director at Princeton High School. The Princeton High School choir is an internationally acclaimed and honored choir.

When I became superintendent, the board suggested I leave it alone and that was good advice. But I did like to watch Bill teach. He was a no nonsense teacher with a wicked and sometimes off-color sense of humor. He usually started class with some sort of joke. Some were good. Some were bad. And some were really awful.

Once the kids were loosened up with his humor, he dove in. They were asked to perform classical works of a very difficult nature. They sang the songs in the original language. Many of the choir kids took more than one foreign language simply so they could better master the language expectations in choir. Every couple of years, they would enter national or international competitions. This gave them something to look forward to and to work toward.

I had the opportunity to travel with the group to Germany and Austria for a festival and competition. Prior to one of the concerts, during the warm-up, Bill was even more outrageous than usual. He was telling joke after joke and bantering incessantly with the students. Just a few days later, just before the major competition, during the warm-up, he was very quiet. He read the words to the song the kids were about to perform (a hymn by Handel), and he talked quietly with them about what the words meant and what Handel was trying to communicate. He asked them to take a few minutes to meditate on it.

Later, I asked him about his very different behavior prior to the two performances. He told me that before the first, he noticed the kids were flat and listless and that he was pumping them up for the performance. For the second one, he realized they were very nervous and uptight, and he used the meditation approach to bring them down to the right level so they were ready to perform. Each time he was trying to bring forth their best selves.

Teachers are not just magicians—they are also conductors. In the case of Bill Trego, that is literally true, but for most, it is figurative. Great conductors pick the right works for the talents of the orchestra or choir. But they also challenge them to exceed what they may think they can do. They bring in all the different parts blending the pieces to create a symphonic outcome. And they understand how to motivate to get the best performance possible. And they find the talent—wherever it might be hidden.

The band director at Princeton was Tony Biancosino. Princeton had a jazz band, and it, too, was award winning. One day, Tony was walking through the school and heard a young man playing harmonica—very, very well. The young man was in the hall because he was skipping class—as usual. Tony asked him why he wasn't in the band. The boy replied all he knew how to play was harmonica. (This was a pivotal moment for that young man. Teachers have the opportunity to grab these moments and change lives. Tony did that.) Instead of letting the young man know he would have to fit the expectation of the band, Tony told him no problem; he would arrange some of the music for harmonica. The boy joined the band and did very well. Tony found out that he was a good singer and arranged songs that allowed him to solo both on harmonica and as a crooner. Tony also discovered that although he was coming to band, he was still ditching his other classes. When Tony confronted him, he told Tony band was the only class he liked. Tony told him that might be so but that was not how it worked. If he wanted to be in the band, he had to do well in all his classes. And while he was at it, he should stop with the pot smoking that everyone knew he was doing. He did go to his other classes, straightened up, and graduated.

The week before graduation, I ran into the young man and asked him what he was going to do after high school. He said, "Doc, I'm going to be a big star." I gave him a half smile and said, "Good for you." I thought he had been lucky to get out of high school. The next time I saw him, he was on the David Letterman Show playing harmonica with the band. That was because the little rock band, Blues Traveler, he had started with some class mates had gone on to sell millions of records. He dedicated their first album to Tony and gave him the subsequent platinum record. Like Lisa's students, he kept coming back, doing benefit concerts to support the band. When Tony was up for a promotion, as he was waiting for the interview, the harmonica player walked in, now the big star he had promised he would be and said, "You just sit there Dr. B. Let me tell this committee why you deserve this promotion."

Teaching is finding that undiscovered gem, setting up the right expectations and conditions and carving it into something precious. When Lisa got to first grade, her class took a trip to a museum. She came home very excited. I asked her why and she told me, "Dad, did you know man came from monkeys?" I asked her how she had learned that, and she told me about what they had seen in the museum including a picture that had a monkey and a bigger monkey and something that looked like a combination of monkey and man and then a man. Of course, she had seen the ascension of man depiction that most adults have seen. Being the typical Princeton parent, I wanted to know all she had learned, so I asked her what that process was called where monkeys became men. She thought for a minute and then brightened and said, "Recycling?" Now aside from the fact she had nailed her understanding of evolution, I thought she had laid out a pretty good understanding of what the process of education was all about.

A number of years ago, I visited the George Washington Carver Museum in Tuskegee, Alabama. Like most Americans, I knew that Carver had been a great scientist, almost single-handedly saving much of the agriculture of the south through his discoveries on the uses of the peanut. What I had not known was that Carver was also an artist. He would take walks along the back roads around the town, and if he found a piece of twine or yarn, he would gather it up and put it in his pocket. If he found an interesting color of clay, he would scoop it up and take it home. When he got enough twine and yarn saved, he would use it to weave tapestries, many of which now hang in museums. When he got enough of the clay, he would use it to paint with, like watercolor paint, and his paintings are displayed in museums around the world. Recycling. In his case, he was taking something of no apparent value and making something priceless out of it.

That is what teachers should be doing every day. Teachers are magicians, conjuring up rabbits out of hats and readers out of little children. They are conductors, pulling the best out of what the students have to give, and they are artists, taking the discarded and disposed of and making something precious from it. The core of education should be to find ways to unleash this potential in our teachers so they can do the same for students.

CHAPTER THREE

Attitude = Altitude

The only way of finding the limits of the possible is by going through them to the impossible.

—Arthur C. Clarke

T he magic of learning is in wanting to learn. People can and will learn almost anything that they want to learn. We spend most of our time and effort in school trying to get children to learn things that we think they need to learn. The key to improving schools and learning is to find a way to get them to *want* to learn what they need to learn. We all know the old saying, "You can get a horse to water, but you can't make him drink." Education rides on the ability of teachers and schools to get the horse to drink. Sadly, this usually entails holding his head under water until he drowns. You can't push a rope, and you can't get the horse to drink unless the horse is thirsty.

The term *motivation to learn* has been defined by Hermine Marshall (1987) as the "meaningfulness, value, and benefits of academic tasks to the learner—regardless of whether they are intrinsically interesting." Ironically, motivation to learn doesn't start at school; it starts at home. Some homes are rich in diverse learning opportunities. Others are bereft of these. If parents nurture the creativity and curiosity in children, their motivation to learn will increase. If children are given the abilities and beliefs such as self-worth, competence, autonomy, and self-efficacy, they will become more willing risk-takers and will attempt more challenging learning opportunities. However, real learning and motivation are affected by school because children get all sorts of signals in school about what kinds of learners they might be. Many signals I got early on were not very positive. School seemed a foreign land with a strange language and customs that I could not understand. I got the signal every time I acted in a divergent fashion that I was not a good student. Sadly, that seems the case for many students.

Teachers have a lot of power over all this. If teachers communicate an expectation that students can and will learn, then amazingly enough, students seem to do so. Various studies have been done that support the Pygmalion effect in classrooms. One study involved the teachers being told certain students were gifted. They were not, but at the end of the term, they were achieving as if they were because the teachers believed in them. After the passage of No Child Left Behind (NCLB) law, President George W. Bush was fond of talking about the "soft bigotry of low expectations." Although I personally have a lot of concern about NCLB, the President was right about the power of expectations. If we expect less out of students, they will never disappoint us. If we expect more, they often surprise us with what they can do. What the President got wrong is that expectations are not everything. Beyond expectations, we have to give them support to meet them. But there is no doubt that expectations are a powerful variable in learning.

The key is to move from the extrinsic models of motivating to more intrinsic ones. Researchers Condrey and Chambers in 1978 found that when students were confronted with complex intellectual tasks, those who had an intrinsic orientation used more logical information-gathering and decision-making strategies than did those who were extrinsically motivated. They also seem to be drawn to more challenging tasks while extrinsically oriented students move toward those with lower degree of difficulty. They found that extrinsically motivated students tend to want to use the minimal amount of effort to get the maximal reward. This seems a recipe for creating lazy and indolent students. It does make one wonder why we continue to use extrinsic methods to reform our schools.

It is not that students can't learn—it's that they don't really want to. All this research came home very powerfully to me based on something that happened to me a few years ago on an educational mission to New Zealand where I visited very exciting classrooms. When our bus stopped at a country store, we found a box of plastic sheepdog whistles for sale. They are the whistles that the farmers use to direct their dogs that in turn herd the sheep. They are a different kind of whistle in that they go inside the mouth. We decided it would be a great thing to learn how to play the sheepdog whistle. We could take a new skill back home. On the first day, everyone could get a sound out of his or her whistle except me. Second day, they were manipulating the sounds, and I was getting nothing out of my whistle. Third day, they were playing, "Mary Had a Little Lamb" and "Twinkle, Twinkle Little Star," and I was just getting spit out of my whistle.

So I started complaining, "Just my luck. I got a defective whistle. I can't take it back and get one that works." And so on. One of the other folks took my whistle and starting playing "Mary Had a Little Lamb," which left me with only one possible conclusion. *I* was the one who was defective. And suddenly, I felt like I had in third grade before Mrs. Spurlock had gotten her hands on me. I started thinking, "What's wrong with me? Why is it so easy for them and hard for me? Why can't I get it?" And I felt embarrassment and shame. And then, in my mind, I did something very interesting. "Who wants to play the stupid sheepdog whistle anyway? I don't have any sheep! I don't even have a dog! I don't care!" You see, we spend a lot of time in school asking ourselves the wrong question—why don't kids want to learn? We should be asking why they want to fail. The answer is pretty clear—they don't. None of us wants to fail. But we keep giving students experiences that put them into failing situations. We keep pointing out what they don't know and what they can't do. Motivation has to be centered on giving kids experiences that connect to their interests and that allow them to feel successful. Failure is a demotivator. Now, initially, I was motivated to learn the sheepdog whistle, but I kept running into failure, so finally, I just wanted to quit.

But I know a few things about my learning style. I am a holistic learner. I have to have all the pieces in place before I get it. And I am resilient. I will not give up, even when faced with failure. That was how I was able to move from slow learner, to underachiever, to gifted. So I didn't stop trying to play the sheepdog whistle. And somewhere late in the third day, all the pieces fell into place, and

I started to get it. My holistic brain stopped acting like it had a hole in it and got it. By that evening, I could do a rough version of "Ode to Joy" on the whistle. I was gifted again! But not all of our children have been given insight into their learning styles, and others have not received the gift of resilience. And if they have experienced too much failure, they throw it in. How many gifted people are out there who, because of the way they were taught or because they were given lessons that didn't connect to them, gave up before they found success? The challenge is for schools to find the right "connectors" for children.

Author Daniel Pink (2009), in his latest book *Drive: The Surprising Truths about What Motivates Us*, points out that the real motivators are not extrinsic, carrots and sticks, nearly as much as they are intrinsic. He suggests that the path to high performance comes from intrinsic rewards. Certainly, if the work is mechanistic and repetitive then external rewards are effective. If you are doing piecework on a factory line, then more production can be rewarded. But if the work is complex and sophisticated an if/then (If I do this, then such and such will happen) approach is counter-productive. This calls for intrinsic rewards such as autonomy, mastery, and purpose. This is very counter to the way we are approaching schools in the era of high accountability. Certainly, if/then methods don't work for creative outcomes. Pink suggests that we will have more conceptual beings if we don't depend on tests to deliver their work. Pink has based his ideas on more than 40 years of research on what motivates people. Despite this, we see an educational system where political leaders are pushing merit pay for teachers, which flies in the face of the research and coercive testing practices to motivate children. It doesn't have to be this way.

Later in the book, when I will tell you about a classroom I visited in Olathe, Kansas, where the students were making robots is a case in point. It was not an easy or frivolous class. They were doing very complex and demanding work. They had to learn very difficult material and had to be nearly perfect in the execution of their work. The students were not swayed by the difficulty of the work. It was just easy for them to connect what they were doing with why it might be important. And they felt a connection to what their interests were. Their motivation was off the charts, and it wasn't because they *had* to do the work. They were drinking deeply from the river of learning because the work connected to them in a deep and powerful way.

When I have been in educational meetings and promoted the idea of learning that gives students learning experiences that are meaningful, I would often get the put-down of "oh, we have to make learning rigorous, if it is going to be meaningful. We have to have high expectations." Yes, we do, but that doesn't mean that it has to be dull and boring. That classroom in Olathe had about as much rigor as I can imagine a class having, and yet the students were totally into it. They were working on a project that connected to their interests—robots and competition. And they were learning why they needed to learn challenging material and skills.

Good education is not rocket science. (Although building rockets might be a good start!) Education is about doing what you are interested in doing. It does not mean that we have to water down the curriculum and spend class singing "Kumbaya." It means we have to spend a lot more time creating classes and curriculums that connect with students. I find it ironic that our students have a rich learning experience—after school is over. They go into an environment that is rich in technology (computers, cell phones, video games, and entertainment), and yet in the hours of school, we tend to give them stifling and boring experiences. The wonder to me has always been not so much why children don't learn, but why they don't rise up and overthrow the schools for giving them such boring and mindless learning experiences. There is no reason school can't have high expectations or require rigorous work. But that has to be connected to the students understanding of why these things are important, and it has to connect to their world and what their interests might be.

The secret to all this is not just the curriculum—it is in the teachers and how they approach the students. If they want the students to stretch, they need to give them the room to do so. Once in Mrs. Sang's Latin class, she asked us to translate "Jason and the Argonauts." I knew the story and had already proven in class that I was pretty good at translating Latin. I decided to "fool" Mrs. Sang by writing a musical based on the story. That would get me out of the more onerous assignment of translating. I spent many more hours writing the musical, and it would have been much less effort to do the original assignment. I thought I had fooled Mrs. Sang, but the joke was on me. She had gotten much more effort from me in a much more creative way than if I had merely translated the story. Good teachers are flexible and allow students to pursue their passions in the interest of the assignment.

But the most important thing a teacher can do to motivate a student is to give them part of themselves. Let me use a word not mentioned much in education circles but which I think is at the core of motivating students—love. I have a friend who was a principal in New York City. They had a new student at her school named Joseph. He was a handful. Shortly after getting to school in the morning, he would run away. So they took his shoes from him in the morning to slow him down. Then they discovered they might have been better off letting him run because his day at school was filled with cursing and hitting. Rather than focusing on his bad behavior, they focused on him as a person. They knew that his mother had recently died and that he and his father were living in a homeless shelter. Joseph's hostility and anger had a real source. So the school gave him what he needed—love. They hugged him, rubbed his head, told him how glad they were to see him every morning, and in the afternoons, they told him how much they were going to miss him. That single ingredient changed Joseph. He stopped hitting. His cursing abated, and he learned to read—all because of the simple act of love.

Later in the year, another new student came to the school. He was hitting and cursing and running away. Joseph pulled the new kid aside one day and told him he needed to start acting better, and if he didn't, he was going to have to "kick his a%#." I guess there are different ways to motivate, and Joseph had not yet learned the power of intrinsic motivation. Later on in the year, another new student moved in, and Joseph decided he would be his new best friend. But he discovered that the new student was deaf and couldn't hear or speak. So Joseph asked the teacher to teach him sign language so he could talk to his new friend. The first sign that Joseph learned was "be good." Joseph had mastered the main lesson. In most things, love is the answer, even if you forgot what the question was. Joseph was just one child transformed by its power, and he had learned what it meant to be good.

We spend a lot of time in school worrying about how to motivate kids. We study the power of extrinsic and intrinsic motivation. As I have said, most of today's reform efforts focus on extrinsic motivation. Yet we know that children are highly motivated before they get to school. It seems what we do to them in school demotivates them. We take children who are intrinsically motivated to learn because they enjoy the activities and the feelings they gain from them, and we start offering rewards and punishment that are external to the activities themselves, thinking that will motivate them. We have to find ways to allow them to use their powers of discovery and curiosity, which are inherent to move them toward success. While attending one of his conferences, I heard Pulitzer-Prize-winning author Frank McCourt say that "education should be an exciting adventure" and that "the human element has to be kept alive in school." As a former high school teacher, he got what motivation is really about—making school an exciting adventure.

CHAPTER FOUR

Leaning Our Ladder Against the Right Wall

We're lost, but we're making good time.

—Yogi Berra

When I was growing up in West Virginia, I was exposed to many colloquial expressions. One that seems most appropriate for looking at education reform is "if you lean your ladder against the wrong wall, you are going to paint the wrong house." When it comes to American education, it seems we are constantly leaning our ladders against the wrong wall. We are misdiagnosing the problems we face, and subsequently, we are developing the wrong solutions. If we want to improve education, we must get the right solutions lined up with the right problems.

We constantly hear from the media and political leaders that the American education system is "broken" and must be "fixed." Schools are "deteriorating," and our children are "at risk" of receiving a third-class education.

This diagnosis is wrong on several levels. First, it presumes that the entire system of schools is failing. Although it is true that many schools are failing, it is equally true that many are doing an outstanding job. It also assumes that *fixing* the current system is the right approach and, finally, that somehow, somewhere else, there is a model of education we should be following that is better than ours and that will serve as a guide for improvement.

Let me take another view. First, the schools of today, overall, are markedly better than those of earlier times. Half a century ago, only about half of the population finished school. Today, we worry about a dropout rate of 10% to 30%. That range is so large because we have varying ways of measuring the problem—a sure way to misdiagnose the situation. If you can't even get your numbers right, it is very hard to get your hands on the problem. From most accounts I have seen, we have between an 80% and 90% completion rate for students. What this means is that when all the alternative methods are considered (GED, community college system), by the time a young person is 25, about 80% to 90% have finished the equivalent of high school. So we haven't deteriorated in high school completion. We have improved.

The problem is that in the mid-20th century, when only half graduated, the other half had a shot at a decent life. Jobs in factories were plentiful and led to a home, a car, and a middle-class lifestyle for the family. Today, there are precious few of those opportunities for the undereducated. The price for failing to complete high school today is huge, so a noncompletion rate of 10% to 20% means millions of young people are entering the adult world without the capacity to make even a minimal living. It also means that the drag they create on our society through incarceration or underproductivity is staggering. We have a problem but it isn't about the schools' declining quality. The problem we have is that the schools haven't kept pace with the changes in our society.

Take another supposed example of school failure such as the relatively flat performance on the SAT exams over the last several decades. This is usually tied to the argument that school expenditures have increased during that time so that schools are failing in their mission (and that money doesn't matter.) However, several studies have shown that during that same time there has been a significant increase in the numbers of students taking the test. In fact, a study conducted by the Sandia Labs (Carson, Huelskamp, & Woodall, 1991) showed that every subgroup taking the test had improved their scores during that time. However, there is a gap in scores where minority and low-income students don't do as well as middle-class Anglo children do. As you get larger numbers of students from these relatively lower-scoring areas taking the test (and even though their performance is improving over time), the *average* drops. This is called, in statistical circles, the *Simpson Paradox* named for the man who first described the phenomenon. The point I am making is that rather than deteriorating, schools are improving. This is best demonstrated by the fact we have made college admission more accessible to our lower classes. The fact that we have a gap in performance is troubling and will ultimately cause us huge problems as our population becomes more minority and expectations for performance increase. But again, the picture is not one of a failed system but one that hasn't addressed emerging problems fast enough.

However, the real issue is that although schools have been gradually improving their performance, the increased expectations of a society that has leaped into the information age, the heightened expectations of work skills, and the deteriorating home and family conditions faced by many students have exceeded this improvement. The issue here is that *we have been making incremental progress in an exponential environment.* So as schools have gradually improved, the conditions around them have strained their ability to keep up. This is not the problem we are working on nationally. So much of what is being offered as current reform ideas suggest we need to do more of what we used to do and do it better. Perhaps we need to focus on what the issues are today and will be tomorrow and create a system that addresses them.

Part of our current angst is that we are not outperforming other countries, as we once did. I am old enough to have lived through a number of these cycles. I remember after Sputnik that we were not educating children as well as Russia—otherwise how would they have beaten us into space? Then we landed a man on the moon, and although the schools were given no credit for this, the uproar died down until the early 1980s when America's economy slipped against Japan and Germany. Again, the schools were the problem, as outlined in the Nation at Risk (National Commission on Excellence in Education, 1983) report. Then as the 1980s moved into the 1990s, Japan and Germany fell back against the roaring U.S. economy, and that quieted the concern until the "Asian tigers" of China and India replaced them. Each "crisis" blamed the American schools. There is no doubt that other countries are doing well. It is not so much because American schools have deteriorated but because others are doing much better. This phenomenon is documented in Fareed Zakaria's (2008) book, *The Post American World*. The reality is that in "the good old days," we had effective schools and ineffective schools. It is just that no one worried much about the ineffective ones because the effective ones were producing enough talent for America to dominate. That is no longer the case. The reality is that schools have not failed in their traditional mission. They have failed to keep pace, which is a very different problem.

This leads to the second assumption—that we need to fix the schools. The fact is that the schools we have are a well-oiled machine doing exactly what they were designed to do. The schools we have are perfectly designed to yield the results we are getting. If we are unhappy with the results, we have a design issue on our hands. You can't fix a bad design. You have to come up with a different design.

Current expectations are that every student will graduate— and graduate with high skills. That is not what the current design was created to produce. The current design, which grew out of the agricultural and industrial revolutions, never anticipated that all students would complete school and, certainly, not do so with very high skills. Schools were supposed to take in large and diverse numbers of students, help them become Americanized, and sort them out for the emerging industrial economy. Some were supposed to be workers and a few managers.

But some of the design predates even the industrial revolution. Take but one example of a vestige of the system left over from the agricultural era—summer vacation. Students were released in the summer to allow them to help with the family farms. School resumed in the fall after the crops were taken in. If you wanted to produce a high-achieving student or to close the achievement gap or to more effectively compete internationally, you wouldn't give students all that downtime to forget what they have just learned. A study conducted at Johns Hopkins University (Cooper, Nye, Charlton, Lindsay, & Greathouse, 1996) showed that for middle-class American students, the summer doesn't seem to have a great impact. Their stimulus-rich home environment allows them to progress over the summer. However, low-income students enter in the fall, actually improve during the year to the point that the achievement gap narrows and then leave for the summer. When they get back, they have lost much of what they had gained the previous year, and the gap has increased. This is a major design flaw in the current system.

Take another major part of the system that grew out of the industrial age, which is the organization of schools around a factory model. Schools built in the 19th and 20th centuries (which are most of them) tend to resemble a factory in physical design: the typical egg-crate model with double-loaded hallways and classrooms on each side holding a certain number of kids in each classroom and each grade. The whole concept of "grade" comes from the industrial model. It is based on the assembly line. Put children on the line; push them through from grade to grade, shoving some knowledge in at each stop, and hope that they come off the line educated people. That is why social promotion has become an anathema—how can you possibly move students along the assembly line if they are missing some parts?

The whole concept of grade level, which dominates the current accountability model, becomes laughable when it is put into this context. What does third grade mean—beyond the stop between second and fourth on the education assembly line? What does "achieving at grade level" mean? It has been shown, and is something every classroom teacher knows through experience, that in a classroom of one grade, there is a wide range of achievement, usually four or five years' worth. How do you fix that? Until we are prepared to redesign the system, top to bottom and side to side, all this talk of fixing makes little sense.

We also hear a lot about how American students don't measure up to children in other countries on international tests. There are several problems with this analysis. Which children are we talking about? America has a more diverse student population than can be found in any other country. Further, the social capital available around the world is very uneven. How does one compare students from a country where basic health care is not necessarily available to those in a place like Scandinavia where it is available prenatal and on? How do you compare the 50 million plus students in the United States with the several hundred thousand in Singapore? Further, how do you compare a largely middle-class country like Singapore with the diversity of Minnesota and Mississippi? Beyond that, how do you compare countries culturally? Asian countries have cultures that are very disciplined and focused on following rules. The American culture is much more independent and challenging of authority.

Thankfully, American students reflect the freedom to be who they want, which is embedded in our culture. How do you compare a country where most mothers are in the workforce with one where most stay at home, focused entirely on their child-rearing duties? How do you compare countries where what is learned and how it is taught varies dramatically with another country? For example, some countries teach physics at an earlier point than the United States. Yet the United States has produced more physics Nobel Laureates than any other country, leading one to conclude that it is less important where you start than where you finish. I started in a substandard school in Davis Creek and ended up at Harvard. Which says more about the American system of education?

Several years ago, I visited Romania just before the results of some international tests came out. The results were focused on high schools, and Romania outperformed the United States. However, having just been there, I knew that after the eighth grade in Romania, students are split between those who are headed for college and those who are not. The non-college-bound students go into vocational training programs—programs where they are not expected to take the international tests. How would the results have been had only the American students who were college bound have taken the test?

The point I am making here is that although it is useful to consider what others countries are doing and how they are going about it, we must do so with some skepticism. Merely taking the results of international comparisons as factual proof that American schools are broken is at best naïve and at worst misguided. Again, it causes us to misdiagnose the problems.

The reality is that the quality of the schools in America has much to do with where they are located. We tolerate a wide variance in support for schools, and we know that many students who lack a middle-class background start well behind the start line. Our nation tolerates a vast gap in social equity between the "haves" and the "have-nots." Other countries have social policies that smooth that out. Some countries allow a much smaller income gap between rich and poor. Our system puts few limits on how rich or how poor a family can be. For example, the single greatest variable in SAT scores is family income. The higher the income, the higher the score achieved.

Today, it is considered politically incorrect to discuss poverty as an intervening variable because we all want all children to succeed regardless of background. However, refusing to acknowledge poverty as an intervening variable for student achievement is like talking about going to the moon and not mentioning the impact of gravity. If we are ever to really redo our schooling in America, a part of that will have to come from smoothing out what Jonathan Kozol (1991) called the "savage inequalities" that are built into the system. How you do should not depend on where you live. And although we do need to heed the call made by former President George W. Bush that we overcome the soft bigotry of low expectations, we have to overcome the hard bigotry of high expectations without adequate resources. Resources alone will not improve schools. Neither will expectations supported by resources inadequate to the challenge.

The fact is that we have some of the finest schools in the world with students who achieve at world-class levels and who constantly perform in wondrous ways. We also have some bad schools where children are daily shortchanged and that exist on the edge of chaos where none of us would want to send our children. And we have schools all along the spectrum in between. If we simply ignore that reality as we call for better performance borders on educational malpractice, we cannot bludgeon our schools to greatness. A simple accountability model applied to a system designed for a different outcome is a form of organized torture.

One of America's greatest challenges is to continue doing what we have always done best—to educate a creative, innovative population. As we have focused the last few years on an accountability model that values test results on norm-referenced, multiple-choice questions, we have begun abandoning the very thing that has made America the envy of the world—our ability to innovate our way out of difficulty. This has increased the pressure on schools as students are living in a digital world but studying in a pencil and paper educational model. The wonder is not that some of our students leave before completing school—the wonder is that more don't leave given the deadly dull experience they often get in school. As we work to improve schools, we need to guard against moving them in the opposite direction of where they need to be going. Quality in the emerging conceptual world will grow more out of motivation and creativity than artificial test results. We need to worry where we are propping the ladder.

We also have a system that was designed for a very different outcome—it was designed to be a place that would house the children, give them some basic skills, and sort them out for the workplace. That is no longer acceptable. Therefore, what is called for is a very different kind of education—one that uplifts students to their highest potential. That means schools will likely look very different from the ones we see today. And it means we will have to start leaning our ladders against the right walls.

CHAPTER FIVE

Crawling Out of the Box

Do what's easy; with any luck at all, it may also be what's right.

—Ashleigh Brilliant

With all the criticism raining down on schools, we often miss the point that the schools of today were designed for a different world. They were created in the context of the industrial revolution and during a time when most of America was still agricultural. Schools dotted the American landscape. They were community organized and community based. They were small with one or two teachers who taught a variety of age levels in one class. There was a long break during the summer to allow students to help on the farm. It wasn't so important that everyone learned. Schools were mostly to teach the basics and, more important, to teach *civic virtue*. Schools were the place where citizens learned to be citizens. They had to have enough skills to do that. Much more was overkill. Schools were not expected to create an intelligentsia or to produce large numbers of highly skilled workers. They weren't needed.

As the nation moved fully into the industrial revolution, the schoolhouse became bigger. This was because we were becoming more urban and we had taken in waves of immigrants. We had to have bigger places to put them. We were also raising the emphasis on education, and more people began taking advantage of its availability. The nation was also becoming more aware of efficiency and began applying the principles of the industrial model to schools. The buildings were no longer the little red one-room schools. They became two or more stories of boxes lining common halls. The bigger buildings also allowed additional activities to be considered. Some had gyms and their own libraries. They were organized around grades, teachers had a narrow age range to teach, and students had to master the material to move on to the next grade. This assembly-line model of education was highly efficient, within limits, and created the opportunity to educate large numbers of students to a modest standard.

In the classroom, students were grouped according to ability. The blue birds, robins, and crows were born. Different schools called them different things, but essentially, you had a slow group, an average group, and a smarter group. As I said earlier, I know a lot about this because I belonged to all three of these groups. As students got older, these informal groupings hardened into tracks.

The top group was expected to move up and on. They were given the best teachers and the fullest curriculum. They were the ones who went on to college and became managers. The others were given as much as possible and were prepped for the factory floor. If there were students who had serious learning problems, they were either pushed out or put in "special schools" away from the regular classes. This system allowed teachers to focus on the students who had potential and to organize the other students to get as much as possible, in the limits of the situation. And it worked pretty well.

Schools produced as many managers as were needed. The really bright students had lots of advantages and filled the elite colleges around the country. State universities had started to grow up to take the ones who couldn't get into more elite schools or who couldn't afford them. The government provided land grants to house these colleges, and larger numbers of American's saw the possibility of college in their future, although the percentage of the total population going on to college was relatively small. The SAT was created as a measure to help determine who should get into the elite eastern schools, and a very small number actually took the test.

After World War II, the nation could not absorb all the returning vets in the workforce, and as a benefit to them and a way of managing the economy, the vets were given support in going on to college, and a much larger percentage of the population emerged as college educated. The economy was booming as pent-up consumerism took hold. America emerged from the war as the only major world economy that had been undamaged by the war. The 1950s became the golden age for America. The middle class blossomed. People started moving into the growing suburbs and leaving behind the cities as places for housing the newly immigrated, not the least of which were the minority immigrants moving from the rural areas of the south where large numbers of workers were no longer needed to the urban areas where a better life might be available.

Up to this point, the schools in the cities were the best in the country. They had the most resources, the best teachers and students, and the economies of scale working for them. As many of the better students' families left for the suburbs and were replaced by students with weaker educational backgrounds and more needs, the urban schools started to decline. Meanwhile, the suburban schools, which were newer and shinier, started getting the best students, as well as more financial and parental support. Funding for public education has always been property tax based, and those with the most valuable property got the most support in taxes. The rural schools declined in numbers and size, and they were just holding on. A new tracking began based on differentiated resources, which were based on where you lived.

The tradition of *local control*, which was very American in concept, meant schools were governed locally and funded locally. There was virtually no federal support or direction for schools. Local boards made the decisions for schools. They were run by superintendents, and each school was led by a principal who organized the teachers in the building and oversaw the learning. People were happy with their schools. The exceptions came in those darker corners of the nation where racial segregation still existed. There, schools were separate and unequal. In 1954, the Supreme Court ruled on Brown versus Board of Education and overturned the formal segregation of schools. The "with all deliberate speed" called for in the ruling took a couple more decades to take shape and for schools to be desegregated. Meanwhile, communities were becoming more segregated because of housing patterns. So as formal segregation was being dismantled, an informal brand was flourishing.

Those affected by the formal implementation of Brown resented the intrusion of the government. As education writer Phil Schlecty (personal communication) has observed, prior to Brown, people thought they had community schools supported by the government (through tax dollars), and after Brown, they had government schools supported by the community. This change in the sense of control created resentment and a loss of support for public schools across the south. In the north, housing patterns were doing what 100 years of formal segregation in the south could not do: create schools that were differentiated by race and social class.

Internationally, America was enjoying an era of dominance, but the world was catching up. As Europe and Japan rebuilt, they started to created inroads into America's economic dominance. Meanwhile, the Cold War was in full force, and Russia was our biggest rival. When Russia launched a satellite into orbit, taking the lead in the space race, Americans were shocked, and blame quickly fell on the schools. As we moved into the 1970s and 1980s and "Made in Japan" was no longer a joke but something to be admired, the blame game continued with education. Schools must be failing the nation if these "defeated" countries were now outstripping us. Delegations were sent to Japan and Germany to observe their schools to see what they were doing that we weren't.

Of course, other things were happening. America put a man on the moon, effectively ending the space race. Nothing was said about America's schools role in that. As the 1980s moved into the 1990s, Japan and Germany fell on harder times, and America reasserted itself economically. Again, the critics were strangely silent.

As the nation entered the new millennium, new threats were noted. The threat of religious extremism started to absorb a large share of the national resources for wars and homeland security. China and India emerged as economic challengers. Disquiet with the schools of America reached new and screeching levels of criticism. More delegations were sent to China and India to see what they were doing in their schools that we needed to emulate. Accountability became the educational watchword. If schools weren't producing enough engineers to compete with the Asian tigers, then we needed to make sure schools were working harder. Tests were ordered, and we declared that we would leave no child behind.

What happened here was actually very simple. The nation changed the goal of education from one where schools were asked to sort workers for the industrial age to begin producing highly proficient workers for the information age. The dirty little secret here was that there were not enough good jobs, even if schools did produce more engineers, and the relatively higher pay rate for workers between the United States and its competitors created a natural imbalance in the competition. If engineers in China are paid one-fifth of what American engineers make, it is difficult to compete economically. And if China and India, with their massive populations, educate only the top 10% of their population, they hold a massive advantage in numbers.

With the ramping up of competition, and with the growing complexity of the workplace, it would no longer be acceptable for *some* of the students to be educated to high levels. Now *all* students would need to be educated to high levels.

This escalation of expectation was appropriate for the changing times. But it ignored two major impediments. As the nation was ratcheting up its expectations, it was not keeping pace with the conditions of families and children. A much larger percentage of children were falling into poverty as the rich became even richer. The "tracking" of earlier times became hardened by economic realities. The SAT test, that old measure for Ivy League readiness, was now being given to a very large proportion of the students in America. A test that was designed for the elite was now the measure for the masses.

The second impediment fed into this. Although we changed our goals for children, we did little to redesign their education. Schools were still locally and state funded with the economic discrepancies implied and built in. Schools were still being built with little attention to the new expectations or reality of the information age and still looking a lot like the factories of earlier days. Suddenly, we were asking that all teachers would be highly proficient without dealing with their training, compensation, or the reality of reasonableness of finding millions of highly proficient teachers to fit into those egg-crated organizations that assumed that every teacher had the right stuff to educate every child to high levels, regardless of their background, social setting, or the support they had at home or when they reached school. The fact that not all our children are reaching high levels of proficiency is built into the current system. To change this requires that we do a major redesign of our schools, our teaching, and how we approach students. It also requires a national realignment in our thinking about how we educate our children.

Thus far, the ideas for reform have done little to change the equation. Conservative reformers have promoted vouchers and charter schools as their major redesigns. Liberals have looked to class size and better teacher pay. The Obama administration has straddled the two by promoting charters *and* merit pay. None of these ideas get at the core need for redesign. Vouchers and charters simply move children around. It is the concept that parental choice will put pressure on the system to change. Competition will force the system into changing. So far, there is scant evidence that children educated via charters do better than those in traditional schools. The reason for that is simple. By and large, you have just changed location. They are still being educated in the traditional ways. Vouchers allow some highly motivated parents to help their children escape poor schools, but they do nothing for changing the basic education they receive. Recent research on charters conducted by Gary Orfield (Frankenberg, Siegel-Hawley, & Wang, 2010) has also indicated that charters increase the problem of racial segregation. Likewise, despite being counterintuitive, research on class size shows no significant improvement with smaller classes. And there is no evidence that merit pay creates better teachers.

Until we accept that a rather radical redesign is called for, we will not see things change. It isn't that the schools have deteriorated—which the critics claim—it is that they have not kept pace with the changing demands and realities. Simply moving children around to force competition begs the real question—are schools, as currently designed, capable of changing the outcomes? Is it really just a matter of forcing competition on schools? Are school people capable of doing more than they are doing and are just in need of outside force to change their ways? Or is the industrial model not the way to educate children for the information age (or the conceptual age promoted by Daniel Pink [2005] in *A Whole New Mind)*?

The concept of *disintermediation* becomes very important here. Disintermediation takes place when a new technology comes on the scene that disintermediates the way things have been done. A good example of this is the Guttenberg printing press. Prior to that time, if people wanted to know what God intended for man, they would go to a priest who would tell them. The clergy held the ability to transfer God's will to man. They were the ones who could read the Bible, which was limited by the fact it was hand copied and in very short supply. Most people could not read and had to take the priests' word for it. Once there was a printing press that could mass-produce Bibles, more people learned to read and had direct access to God's word. This led to the reformation and changed history forever.

The new technologies that are readily available to parents have changed (disintermediated) education. Children no longer have to go to school to access learning. Software and the Internet make for a very rich curriculum available to everyone who can get to a computer. The role of school must, by definition, change under these circumstances. Clayton Christensen (2008) in his book *Disrupting Class* predicts that by 2020, half of all students will be educated via technology rather than in classrooms. This is disintermediation on steroids.

If this is true, what role, if any, does formal schooling have? I believe there is still a place for the softer side of education. Machines have not yet mastered what it means to be human. Habits of the mind have to be demonstrated and taught. Social skills are gained in social settings. Learning to tolerate and appreciate different value systems and thinking can best be gained by being with other people. It is difficult to teach tolerance at a computer. So the new design for schools would incorporate the modern with the ancient.

So what would this design look like? Well, first, it will incorporate much more use of brain research and technology than we currently use. Both of these will be addressed in subsequent chapters. It will also hark back to the early days of education when schools were seen as places for civic virtue. Ironically, the little-red schoolhouse that had only one or two classes provides a real clue into the future. The pedagogy of those days was teacher centered and rigid. Students used the McGuffey readers, the Bible, and little else to study from. But different ages were in the same class, and students who could progress, did so regardless of age. Students helped one another, and the teacher often acted as a guide to learning.

Now, imagine that model with education using technology and understanding learning styles to personalize learning, allowing for progress regardless of age or ability. Imagine students of different ages working together, with the younger ones benefiting from the older ones' knowledge and skills, and the older ones benefiting from the need to organize what they know and demonstrate it to other children. Imagine school being the entire community with learning taking place in a variety of settings.

Imagine a school where not every teacher is expected to be a master teacher—where teaching is differentiated along with the learning. There is no reason to believe that we can have millions of teachers who are outstanding—where every one of them is world class. There is no other profession where this is true. We have doctors and lawyers of varying competence. Not all plumbers are created equal. Why should we expect that we can overturn the laws of nature and make every teacher Socrates?

The truth is that we have many great teachers in the classrooms of America—there are many Mrs. Spurlocks, Miss Reynolds, Mr. Balls, and Mrs. Sangs out there—teachers who may not be master teachers but who make a difference in children's lives. Further, there are teachers like Mrs. Van Ness and Mr. Trego who are truly master teachers, and there are many of those out there as well. But there are more who are just average. What happens if we accept this reality but redesign learning so that the master teachers are not only put in charge of larger groups of students but also assisted by the not so masterful? We would ensure that all children have some access to the best. We could truly differentiate the compensation for teachers, paying the masters more, not for their test scores but for the recognition of their added responsibilities and workload and ability to inspire students. We could also have interns assigned to each large group. They could learn from both the professional teachers and the master teachers, and this could increase the numbers of competent adults available to all students. This would require looking at creating teams of teachers and students with differentiated roles, but with the goal of personalizing student learning by offering meaningful instruction. Creating schools that students want to go to and that involve meaningful engagement would not be a bad place to start in getting out of the boxes we have created. It could be the easiest and most right thing we can do.

CHAPTER SIX

How It Ought to Be

You see things; and you say, "Why?" But I dream things that never were; and I say, "Why not?"

—George Bernard Shaw

On my visits to other countries, I have often thought that although American critics like to trash American public schools, we still have the best education in the world. I had never seen a classroom in another country that I would trade with an American classroom—until that day, and the subsequent days I spent in New Zealand. What I witnessed was students engaged in meaningful learning activities. Their motivation was off the chart, and their focus on the work was stunning.

I stepped into the classroom, which was buzzing with the excited voices of children. The room was filled with the color of student drawings on the walls and papier-mâché sculptures. I noticed most of the students were in stocking feet. Some were curled up in beanbag chairs reading. Others were sitting on the floor. Desks were shoved all around the room, and as student groups formed and reformed, the desks went with them. It was like watching a giant amoeba at work. There was a blur of movement as students walked or trotted from one place to the other. The whole place smacked of the chaos that some critics level at schools—disorderly, noisy, and no one in charge. In fact, I couldn't even find the teacher myself. This classroom marked the first of several I visited during my stay in

New Zealand, a country known for orderliness and educational innovation. This classroom didn't seem so orderly or innovative. But my first impression was wrong—dead wrong.

I finally spotted the teacher sitting in the floor with two or three students engrossed in a project they had undertaken. She was guiding and supporting them in their work, and they were totally involved. We hear that teachers should be a guide on the side and not a sage on the stage. Well, here it was in action. But what about the other kids? This was great for the few getting her attention, but chaos seemed to be reigning in the rest of the class. But as I focused on individuals and the small clusters of noisy children scattered around the class, I realized that each of them was just as engrossed and engaged as those working with the teacher. They all had their projects and activities. Some were being done alone, with the child working on an individual activity. They were the quiet ones, and they were totally oblivious to the tumult that surrounded them. They were writing or researching a project or making charts and drawing to illustrate their work. Most of the class was working in smaller groups with lots of give-and-take between the students and the occasional foray of an emissary sent to another group. They were seeking advice or offering consultation. I quickly realized that to my eyes, which were used to teacher-centered, student-response classrooms, I was seeing something entirely different. I was watching a whole room full of kids totally absorbed in the learning process with the teacher playing a very different role than I was used to seeing. What I had mistaken for chaos was a class where students knew what they needed to do and were going about it in a purposeful way.

This scene reminded me of a project created and conducted by a group of middle school teachers in Princeton. They set aside several weeks of the year for the project and much of the school was involved. They divided the kids into "countries." They had to set up a government, create an economy, and conduct diplomacy and business with other countries. The kids were more engaged for those few weeks than they were for the rest of the year. They loved taking on the roles and seemed oblivious to the deep learning they were mastering about how governments worked and how economies were created. Some of the countries failed. Others succeeded, and the kids had to do a postmortem to determine why and how that had happened. This was all before education in America became all about test results.

I have always believed in this era of school reform that most of what we were doing in America was off target. We have been trying to use assessment and standards to drive learning. The problem with that is that you cannot beat people to success by making them fearful of the outcome. Assessments are useful as tools for the teacher and administrator to detect the efficacy of curriculum and the outcomes of what is being tried. Standards give a sense of direction; both are necessary but insufficient to producing learning at a high level. What has to happen in a classroom is that students have to see that the work they are doing is important to them, and it has to get their brains off the seat and moving— much of what I witnessed in that New Zealand classroom.

We have also seen reform aimed at structural changes—charter schools, vouchers, or small high schools. As I have already said, none of these touches the heart of what happens in the learning process. Learning is a series of relationships. The most critical is the student-to-student relationship, where they learn to deal with one another, learn from one another, and respect one another. The second most important is the relationship between the student and the teacher, where children are asked the right questions, given the right encouragements, and supported in their work. The next is the relationship from teacher to teacher, where teachers learn from one another and supplement one another's insights and skills. The fourth key relationship is that between the school and the community. This gives the school support and a place for learning to take place, and it gives the community insight about its children, how they can be supported, and how important they are to the future. The final and most central relationship is that of the student to what is being taught. This allows students to work on meaningful and engaging activities that motivate and inspire them and give the background they need to succeed. Any reform has to address all these relationships to be effective. Changing governance, structures, or setting different standards won't touch these relationships.

The fundamental difference between school reformers is the assumptions made about the learning process. Most reform today assumes that learning can be *invoked* into the student and the best reform is the one that does the best job of invoking learning. It is like that model of Mrs. Spurlock who used the end of her yardstick applied to the top of my head—it should open the mind to learning possibilities. Well, this is one place where Mrs. Spurlock had it wrong. Sticks are poor motivators, and learning can't be forced into a child. My learning came from her caring for me, her making certain my parents were involved in the process, and my learning the love of what was in the books. Learning cannot be *invoked* in students—it must be *evoked*. It goes back to the core meaning of the word "educate," which in the Latin is *"educare,"* which means to bring forth. The best classrooms are places of evocation where students create the meaning of the lesson and internalize it for future use.

Television comedian Jay Leno has made a career out of his "Jay Walking" sequences where he asks people on the street answers to simple questions they should have learned in school. The humor comes not just in their not knowing the answers to the basic academic questions but that they often know the answers to questions that are similar but trivial. They don't know who the Chief Justice of the Supreme Court is but can name the lead singer for the Supremes. The recent TV hit show, "Are You Smarter Than a Fifth Grader" plays off the same theme. We see the children out-shining the adults on the show. If nothing else, that should put a lie to the criticism of America's schools because the kids seem pretty smart, but it doesn't really because the adults who are so dumb are also products of the schools. The irony here is that with search engines as close as our fingertips playing this endless game of Trivial Pursuit is unnecessary. Facts are all around us. What is less prominent is the ability to make knowledge and wisdom out of these random bits of information.

Are American adults really that stupid? Yes and no. Yes, in that they are stumped by questions that young children can easily answer. But no, in that I suggest those young children, in a few years, won't be able to answer the questions either. Why? Because learning has been poured into them so they could answer the questions on a test, but as soon as the test is over, they no longer need to know the answers, and they are quickly forgotten. They know the answer in fifth grade but not at 50. We tend to remember those things that are important to us and forget the rest. It is a very efficient use of our brainpower. The key is to make certain that those things that are important to society are important to students and that can only come though the creation of meaningful and engaging learning situations.

After the most recent educational summit between governors and business leaders, I had the occasion to visit a classroom in Olathe, Kansas. First, I have always found it amusing that we have summits on the quality of education led by elected officials and business titans who presumably know more about the making of laws and money than they do the creation of learning. They never seem to want to involve educators in the discussion—a major oversight, it would seem. Consequently, their solutions seem a bit simplistic and naive. (Given the chaos of our current business climate and the overall ineffectiveness of government, perhaps we need a summit on those problems led by educators! But I digress.) This particular summit was on the quality of American high schools, and they concluded that they needed to be reformed. Big surprise! The reality is that America has some of the best high schools in the world and probably some of the worst and a lot in between. Perhaps we should be looking at those schools that are already vibrant learning places as the guidepost for what the others should look like before we head off in a new reform direction.

I found this amusing because we have been reforming high schools virtually from the time they were created, and they haven't seemed to reform. I think that is because we have yet, as a nation, to decide what high schools should do and be about. Are they places of preparation for life? Getting into college? Are they places where the final touches are put on students? Are they holding pens for teenagers that the public would prefer not to see on the street? This summit didn't answer these questions either, but the participants decided that what we needed were more courses and harder courses and more tests and harder tests. This *more* and *harder* approach has been the bulwark and has been tried for the last 20 years of school change, but it is not so true because it has not brought the desired results. It has been the underpinning of school reform since the Nation at Risk report (National Commission on Excellence in Education, 1983). Ironically, in the 20-year period between the time that report was issued and 2003, we increased the average number of Carnegie units required in high school from 21 to 26 (more), and we have increased the number of high schools offering advanced-placement courses (harder) from 5,000 to 14,000. Further, the number of students taking the advanced-placement tests (harder) increased from 200,000 to nearly 1.6 million (more). Another study I ran across set during that same period asked students if they found high school meaningful or useful. In 1983, 40% found it meaningful, and 51% found it quite useful. By 2003, those numbers fell to 28% and 39% respectively. One must worry that if the political leaders and business titans get their way, schools in the future will be very hard and very long and lacking in any meaning or usefulness.

The leader of the summit, a Fortune 500 CEO, was interviewed by USA Today, and he opined that if America didn't start doing a better job of producing engineers, he was going to have to start outsourcing those positions in his company to other countries. I am sure the relative cost of engineers between America and a country like India would have nothing to do with that decision.

With that entire buzz, I was scheduled to visit Northwest High School in Olathe, Kansas, the next day. The school system had developed a 21st-century high school program there, and they invited me to visit. The program was supposed to be a tech-prep program, preparing students for the world of work after high school. Because my own tech-prep experience consisted of soldering little metal boxes and making other little boxes out of wood, I was anxious to see what they were doing.

We walked into one of the classrooms, and the place was electric. Students were involved in different parts of the room, and the excitement level was off the charts. It seemed to be a high school version of that classroom in New Zealand. The teacher stopped the class and asked one of the students to tell the visitor (me) what they were doing. He told me they were building "Battlebots," which are little robot devices that are used in competitions. They "battle" each other with hammers and the like, and the last "bot" standing wins. It is sort of a demolition derby for robots. After telling me this, he must have seen something in my face. He said, "Now you might think this is frivolous, but this is serious stuff."

He, with other members of the class chiming in, proceeded to explain all the metallurgy they had to learn to create the shell that would withstand so many hundred pounds of pressure, as the hammers of the other bots would be pounding on their creation. Then they started explaining how they had engineered the frame to handle the mechanics and the pounding. Then they proceeded to talking about the drivetrain and the robotics, and I must admit, they lost me. I may be smarter than a fifth grader, but not nearly as smart as a high school tech-prep student. I was lost.

About that time, a student rushed up to me holding something, and he had this ear-to-ear grin on his face. "And this is the insulation that goes between the shell and the frame. And we invented this. We are getting a patent on it. No one else has it but us." His pride in the creation of the insulation and the work they had done was mirrored by the entire class. I was seeing innovation at work.

Having just read about having all our engineering jobs outsourced to India, I asked them if any of them were planning to go to college. Every hand went up. Then I asked if any of them were planning to go into engineering. Again, every hand went up. I had to conclude that apparently there was no shortage of engineers in Olathe, Kansas, because the schools had found a way to make their learning meaningful and engaging.

At that point, I asked the student why he was so excited. He said, "In my other school, they told me I needed to learn calculus because it was good for me. Now, I know why I need it. I had to use it in this project." Once again, I had a testimony for meaningful and engaging learning.

When I was superintendent of schools in Tucson, Arizona, I worked with Paul Heckman, a professor at the University of Arizona. We were discussing school reform and how it should be approached. He had proposed taking our lowest-scoring school and doing a project that would work with the teachers in a different way and focus education in a different way. Paul conducted weekly seminars with the teachers, worked with them to make their classrooms places of real learning, and developed methods for involving the parents in the learning process. I remember visiting the school one day when one of the mothers, who spoke no English, was helping the kids make tortillas. Her child beamed with pride, and instead of being ashamed of his mother because she spoke no English, he was the center of attention because she was a master tortilla maker.

In one of my many conversations with Paul, he said something I have always considered profound. He said, "You know, if Lute Olsen (the Men's Hall of Fame Basketball coach at Arizona) did basketball the way we do school, the players would get together every afternoon, and they would read books about basketball, they would write papers about basketball, and they would discuss basketball. They would just never play basketball!"

I was stunned. He had hit the problem dead on. We give children all sorts of *reflected* learning activities (reading, writing, talking), but we rarely give them real activities. They never get a chance to try out their intellectual muscles and do the real work of what they are learning. That elementary classroom in New Zealand and that high school classroom in Kansas had broken that mold. The students were really working on the work. That is the direction we need to take as we talk about reforming schools. It isn't so much that we need a reform strategy as we need one that *transforms* the learning process from the passive, receptive invoked model to an active, creative evoked approach to learning. That would take us a long way down the path toward real learning. And it would motivate the students.

CHAPTER SEVEN

Getting Kids Ready for Democracy

Public education does not serve a public, it creates a public.

—Neil Postman

Most Americans do not realize that the original purpose of public schools was not to teach reading, writing, and arithmetic. Those were goals, but the first and most important goal, as I have already pointed out, was to teach civic virtue. The founders of our country realized that democracy was hard work and that only an educated populace could sustain it. Although at the time of the founding most citizens were white, Anglo Saxon Protestants, there was almost an intuitive sense that, eventually, this would be a country of diversity. Certainly, we already had many former African residents, who, at the time, were given less status as citizens—that is the ones who were not slaves outright. We also had a large native population that had mostly fled west. But the nation was built from immigrants—people who had fled tyranny to find opportunity. It was clear that, as the country filled up, it would look different. By the time public schools were actually created in the 1800s, we had already seen waves of immigrants from other parts of Europe. How were we to incorporate them and make them citizens? The task was given to public schools to teach these new Americans how to appreciate the gift of democracy and how to contribute as citizens.

As our country has modernized, the schools were given more and more to do, but at the core, it was still the expectation that schools would teach citizens how to be citizens. One of the greatest challenges to schools now, as I stated earlier, is the *disintermediation* of education. Today, the power of technology makes information instantly available to anyone. Parents have access to online curriculum, and students have the net world available for their searching. This has disintermediated the schools by changing the relationship of schools to the public. Schools are no longer the intermediary for learning. Children no longer need to go to a place called school to become educated. In the long term, this calls into question the very existence of schools as institutions. However, there remains a very important role for schools, and it is the one that was originally given to them—the creation of citizens. Despite all the advances to social-networking technology, nothing has replaced the power of face-to-face discussion and having to rub up against someone who holds different views and values than you. Schools have been a historic place to allow this to happen.

Several years ago, the Cato Institute issued a report blaming public schools for causing much of the social conflict in our country. The report focused on the fact that there was a lot of conflict in public schools. It is certainly true that there is a lot of social conflict in and around schools. That is true because they are the place that the differing values in our society meet. In fact, they don't create conflict so much as serve as a place where it can be resolved. Blaming public schools for conflict is like blaming the police for crime or the fire department for fires. Because a democracy in a diverse country can be a boisterous and rowdy affair because of the differing views and values, it is important to have a place for these to be explored and resolved. Historically, one of those major places has been our public schools. The author of the report failed to understand this is one of the basic reasons to have public schools. It is much better to have the verbal conflicts that exist in schools than the shooting conflicts that we see around the world in countries that have not yet figured out how to sort through their differences. In fact, one of the major recommendations of the 9/11 Commission that looked into how to prevent another 9/11 was that America should support the development and growth in public schools in the Muslim world so that young Muslim students could grow up with a better way to resolve their differences and could learn the moral power of democracy.

Sadly, the last few decades have seen some decline in the focus on citizenship in our country. One of the unintended consequences of the high-stakes testing reforms is that they have squeezed other things out of the curriculum so that things that might be taught have been marginalized in favor of those things that could be tested. For example, there is not a test for how to be an effective citizen. So the teaching of citizenship has taken a back seat. Further, the very conflicts that prove the worth of teaching students how to be citizens have jeopardized the teaching of citizenship. Schools have shied away from teaching citizenship values for fear of further conflict. I would argue that if schools are to survive and thrive in the disintermediated world of advanced technology, it will come through embracing the human side of the work. Rather than reducing courses and activities in these areas, schools should be upping the ante and placing a greater emphasis on face-to-face interaction, service learning, character education, and engagement in civic activities.

Some of the most powerful learning that is taking place in education today is actually happening outside of schools, such as service projects and public engagement that some schools now require of students.

Service learning is a relatively small but growing movement in the United States. I became familiar with it when I was superintendent in Princeton, New Jersey. We allowed and encouraged a small group of teachers to develop service projects for students. In fact, each student in the program was assigned a person to help or a classroom of younger children to support. My daughter read to a blind senior citizen. She later told me it was the best thing she had learned at school—how powerful and rewarding it was to help someone else.

There has been some controversy as to whether service learning should be required or whether it should be voluntary. I side with requiring it. Children learn to love many things by being required to do them, and many discover it is something they like doing, but probably never would have tried on their own. When I was working in Birmingham, Alabama, we developed a gifted project that pulled students from all the high schools for a semester into a central setting. A piece of the program required them to spend a few hours a week in a service project. They vehemently protested. They explained that they were gifted students and were too busy to go around helping someone else. We explained to them that as gifted students, we fully expected them to take their appointed place as leaders someday, and serving others is at the core of sound leadership. And besides that, the grant we had received had that element in it, and we couldn't change it.

With all the moaning and groaning they did around the project, we did follow-up studies with them to see how the program had affected them after they returned to their home high schools. We found that almost all of them had continued their service project even though it was no longer required. We asked some of them why, and as my daughter found years later, they indicated that they had found great joy and satisfaction in serving others, and they liked how it made them feel. They had drunk deeply from the water we had forced on them and found it refreshing.

A few states, such as Maryland, have required service as a part of their graduation requirements. I talked with the former Lt. Governor of Maryland Kathleen Kennedy Townsend, who had helped make this a reality. She explained to me that, being a Kennedy, she had been raised with a very strong family ethic that assumed a life of service to others, and she wanted to see it spread to the next generation. The reality of service is that when one serves, they are served themselves. When Kathleen's uncle, Senator Ted Kennedy, died in 2009, Vice President Biden suggested that one of the most powerful things about him was that it had never been about him; it had always been about the other person. Senator Kennedy had lived out that family ethic that Kathleen described. Service learning creates a new golden rule. Whatever you do for others, you are also doing for yourself. It is hard to have a country where the citizens have not learned this powerful lesson. Serving others is one of the best things a citizen can do as a requirement for citizenship.

Another major part of getting kids ready for democracy is allowing them to do the real work of making the world a better place. A wonderful example of this actually came from a movement started in Australia based on the Aborigine custom of a *walkabout*. In the Aboriginal culture, young people, before entering adulthood, have to go on a six-month walkabout experience in the bush. At the end, they return to their tribe as an adult—or they die in the experience. (And we thought high-stakes testing was tough!) They have to use all the skills they learned as children to make it through this ordeal. At the end of the process, if they make it, they are declared an adult.

The educational walkabout program was created and championed by Maurice Gibbons, who was struck by the walkabout experience for young Aboriginals compared to the passage to adulthood in the white culture. The young natives have to face a life-threatening but appropriate experience to prove they are ready for adulthood. All the things they face in those six months call on the skills they will need throughout their lives. On the other hand, children in the developed world are faced with a barrage of tests that have little to do with the issue of survival beyond earning a diploma and, perhaps, admission into a college. This practice reflects reality but doesn't offer real experience in dealing with it. Students have to analyze problems, but they never get a chance to solve them in unfamiliar but real experiences.

A major part of the experience of the young Aborigine is that it is a solitary experience, which not only calls on the youth's physical skills but also requires an inward journey of spiritual reflection. It gives him a chance to know himself. In the developed world, our students are forced into being part of a crowd and never have to confront their inner questions directly. They never have to face the "dark night of the soul" that comes from personal crises and challenge.

In a seminal article published in Phi Delta Kappa magazine in 1974, Gibbons posits what a comparable walkabout might look like if we chose to apply it to students in North America. He suggests that it should meet several criteria. It should be experiential and real and not simulated. It would be like the way Coach Olsen did basketball—having the players play it rather than reading about it. It should also be a challenge that pushes the capacities of the students so they could see the self-imposed limitations that they believe are merely barriers to be broken. It should be a bit risky and extend the talents they already have. And perhaps most important, it should be a challenge that students choose for themselves—not one imposed by teachers or others. It should also be an important learning experience. The students need to break out of the trivial that has been imposed on them by others. It should count for something. And finally, it needs to be appropriate to the needs of the student and to society. Gibbons goes on to describe what this might look like in our world. He suggests that the activity should combine adventure, creativity, service, practical skill, and logical inquiry.

In the Birmingham gifted program, we tried a walkabout activity by requiring the students to take on an action project. They had to identify a specific problem in the community and then had to create a project to solve the problem. They had to apply the skills they already had to this real and meaningful activity. One of the students was able to write a bill around her project to deal with a specific environmental issue. She had to research all aspects of the issue and then work on how she could make a difference around it. Her plan was to get a bill introduced into the state legislature to deal with the issue. She testified to the legislative committee on behalf of the bill, and she was able to see it introduced and passed. Another student started a local project to clean up a certain neighborhood. He had to work through all the logistics and politics to get it done. In fact, all the students were exposed to the political process. We had the mayor and members of the city council speak to them. The students observed council meetings. They attended court trials. It was a real crash course in Citizenship 101. I am convinced that if I could find these students now, years later, if they are not acting as leaders, they are powerful contributing citizens in their community.

Embedded in all this learning is the need to teach values. Again, because of controversy and court decisions, many schools have danced around the *V* word. Immediately, you get into a discussion over *whose* values to teach. It isn't that hard. From a spiritual perspective, there is huge overlap between the values of the various religions. But you can start with civic values. We know from the laws that have been passed that certain things are expected of all of us: respect for rights and property of others and the necessity not to harm another. That is a good place to start.

Again from my time in Birmingham, we asked the school board to pass a set of values that would be the guiding principles for the district. We had our own television station for the district. We developed a series of programs that taught the values, and we had a teacher's guide to go along with the program. One of the programs was on honesty. The show involved a student who found a billfold, and there was a discussion among her friends as to what she should do about it. It was brought out that it was not hers and the best thing to do was turn it in. One of the friends pointed out that "finders keepers, losers weepers" should be considered. Another pointed out that possession is 9/10 of the law. A rich discussion ensued.

Another lesson on respecting others involved a magic mirror. Someone would appear in the mirror, and the students would discuss whether they liked that person based on how he or she looked. Then they got to meet the person who they thought was "mean" because of the frown on his face and found that he was actually going through a family tragedy and that is why he looked unhappy. The bottom line to this lesson was that you can't always tell a book by its cover and that we need to suspend judgments of others until more facts are in.

Nationally, there are a number of wonderful programs to get at this issue of character building. The Character Education Partnership has identified a number of good programs. Character Counts (2010), a program created by Michael Josephson, lays out six pillars of character that schools should be teaching. They are (1) trustworthiness, (2) respect, (3) responsibility, (4) fairness, (5) caring, and (6) citizenship. Rushworth Kidder has developed a program for teaching ethics that has similar expectations. Peter Yarrow, of Peter, Paul, and Mary, has developed a program called Operation Respect that teaches kids to be more accepting and respectful of others. The point here is that there are many programs available to schools that can get them around their fears of controversy. Each of these programs has been tested in schools and has found wide acceptance. Teaching values and character are at the core of what schools should be about, and it can be done, even in an age of conflict and controversy.

The bottom line is that in the future the schools must play a central role in bringing people together and teaching the young how to navigate their way through our democracy as well as through life. This will require character, a sense of service, and real skills tested in meaningful ways.

CHAPTER EIGHT

Getting Kids Ready for School— Raising the Village

How are the children?

—Masai greeting

When I was superintendent in Tucson, we had a governor who was impeached. He was followed by a governor who was sent to prison, making Arizona a state for the gubernatorially challenged. The one who was impeached brought a man who had been in the state legislature into his office to be his education adviser. He had completed the eighth grade and had been a longtime advocate for "creationism" in schools—making him the perfect education adviser, I suppose. Because he could no longer introduce his creationism bill, he had a friend do so, but he testified on its behalf. In his testimony, he said that schools have no right to teach anything parents don't want taught. One of the legislators asked, "Do you mean that if the parents think the Earth is flat, the school has no right to teach them differently?" He said, "Absolutely." Of course, the next day the papers were buzzing about the governor's education man who thought the earth was flat.

That day, a reporter came to see me and asked what I thought about the "flat earth" situation. I was in one of those playful moods that screamed, "Not a good day to talk to the press," but there she was so I said, "I'm very concerned. I have 60,000 kids I'm responsible for. What happens if one of them walks over to the edge and falls off? I have safety issues to consider and liability questions to think about. This is serious!"

She said, "Now, do you really think that the earth is flat?"

I opened the drapes to my window and pointed out to the sidewalk and parking lot. "Look at that. I don't know why I never noticed it before."

Continuing the tongue-in-cheek dialogue, or in my case the foot-in-mouth responses, she asked me the question all superintendents get on a daily basis. "What are you going to do about it?" I told her that I had given it some thought. I was going to ask the community for donations of parachutes. That way we could equip the children with parachutes, and if they fell off the edge, they could just pull their ripcords and float down.

She asked me if she could get a picture of me standing in front of a globe. I told her that I had sent all the globes to the warehouse to have them flattened and we didn't have any in the office. The next day the front page of the paper had a headline, "Houston Fears for Student Safety." My friends got me a T-shirt that said, "Get Your Chute Together."

This is a true story that, among other things, demonstrates the danger of talking to the press when you are in a playful mood. But it also shows the kinds of controversies schools get into on topics that have no educational value. It depicts the expectations that no matter what the problem, the school leader is expected to "do something" about it. It also shows the willingness I had as a superintendent to engage the community in solving problems my students faced, which is really the only way school problems can truly be handled.

There is a famous African proverb that educators love to quote: "It takes a village to raise a child." This strikes at the heart of the challenge for educators. The task of educating can only be done successfully if there is a team working on the challenge. Schools are tasked with the central mission of educating—that is why parents send their children off each morning. But education does not take place in a vacuum. If the child is sick, abused, or ill prepared, the school is rolling the rock uphill in trying to overcome these issues. It takes parents and the broader community to help. But often in today's world, those elements are missing. So when educators want to quote the proverb, they need to ask a follow-up question: "What does it take to raise a village?" In modern society, the village is as antiquated as stagecoaches and buggy whips. Children are growing up today in a world lacking in the web of support that is necessary for success.

That means the first task of a school is to shoulder the burden of remaking the village. This is the only way real success is possible. But schools also exist at the physical and psychological center of communities. If you walk through most communities, it won't take you long to find a school. Historically, most communities were either built around a school or the school was placed in the center of the community. Initially, that was so children could walk to school. As communities grew, or desegregation plans were undertaken, it meant that children would be bused to school but the "centeredness" of the school prevails to this day. Also, the school is often the place where other activities occur. In the case of older children, the music and drama productions and the sports programs draw the community to the school. So the school has been at the physical center of communities, and they have also occupied the social and psychological center. Although society has changed, the school is still there, and it could be used as a magnet for creating a more vibrant village. But often, schools have not taken full advantage of that central location. Historically, educators viewed their work as *their* work, and the community was kept at arm's length. That has started changing, but most schools are still not using their centrality as a means of creating a stronger community. How might they do that, and what should be happening?

First and foremost, school folks need to help bring people together. I used to have a little joke sign in my office that said, "The time for action is past, and now is the time for senseless bickering." I finally put the sign away because so many communities are caught up in all sorts of controversy, and they need no encouragement to do senseless bickering. From fights over books in the library or curriculum to differences over coaches or who made the cheerleading squad, there are far too many adult agendas being played out around the school. It would be good to remember the less-well-known African proverb that speaks beautifully to this: "When the elephants fight, the grass gets trampled." In today's world, we have far too many children being trampled because the focus is on the adults rather than the children. Being a school person in today's world requires that you be a peacemaker. The first step toward creating a village is raising the awareness of everyone that the children are the central client and that adult agendas undermine that crucial work. We need a sign that quotes the infamous Rodney King: "Can't we all just get along?"

School people are often the biggest culprits in these battles. I have sat in far too many faculty meetings and through too many school board meetings where every item of the agenda was centered on adult concerns: teaching schedules, lunchroom duty, teacher contracts, staff hiring or firing, and so on. Although many of these things need to be addressed, when they become the center of the work, then something very important is getting lost—a focus on children. So when it comes to creating a community, educators must start with the notion from medicine: "Physician, heal thyself." Peacemaking starts in the school. From there, it is much easier to bring parents and the broader community in and help them work together.

My reputation as a superintendent was as a "healer." When I arrived in one particular community known for its epic battles over the schools, a television interviewer laid out a long litany of controversies in the community and asked me the "gotcha" question, "How are you going to heal this mess?" My answer was simple. "My job isn't to heal the problems here. My job is to create the conditions so that the community can heal itself." School leaders must be in the "healership" business. That simply means—don't be the source of the conflict and work to allow the people who care most about the schools—the parents and community—find ways to work together for the benefit of the children.

That leads naturally to the next step—opening up the school to the broader community. First, we must make schools more parent friendly. Schools should do periodic checks on how friendly they are. One idea used by some is to do an annual customer survey that asks people a series of questions around this issue. Community checkups are revealing and give a great sense of what the school can do to bring the community closer. The mere act of asking their opinions even creates a more positive feeling for the school.

I have known some principals or superintendents to have a friend, not known to the staff, come to the office to see how they are treated. In today's post-Columbine world, schools have, by necessity, closed in to protect children from possible harm. But some schools have been able to do this without creating a fortress-like environment. I have sometimes joked that rather than doing school reform, we are doing *reform school* (metal detectors, uniforms, and guards). If a school looks a lot like a prison and feels like a prison, the students will begin to act like prisoners.

A superintendent friend of mine told me that in his former district, the school board bought plans for a prison and used them to build their high school. They saved some money on architecture fees, but I have no idea what that communicated to the community and what it cost them in creating a learning environment that was welcoming, but I can imagine what it said to the students. It is doubtful that we have really made the children that much safer, and by creating a prison-like atmosphere, we have done terrible damage to the work that should be going on in schools. We should not create schools as places where parents feel like they are going for visitation or where we are fearful of their bringing in a hacksaw hidden in the cupcakes so they can break out their children. One simple thought would be to create a school environment that we would want for our children and one where we would feel welcomed.

For parents, I strongly believe we need to go further. It is not just a matter of making them feel welcomed. It is a matter of using their natural interest in their children to enhance the learning environment and helping them be more effective parents. I have always found it amusing that we teach students driver's education training but we don't give them parent education training, which is a much more complex and important role. We should make certain that in the middle or high school curriculum or in the health classes that most schools require a portion is dedicated to basic parent training. They should be given a basic understanding of child development and ways parents can work with children to help them learn. For many students, this is something they will need down the road, but for too many, it is something they will use too soon, as teenagers are having children often before they graduate.

I also think schools should provide training for current parents. In several of the districts where I worked, we created a

Parent Academy that offered classes in dealing with such things as understanding your teenager and sibling rivalry. These classes were welcomed by the parents and bonded the district to the parents. Parents were eager for the support, and the school bene-fited by having parents who were better at their jobs, which natu-rally made our job easier. In Riverside, we went so far as to have a class for African American parents helping them understand the unique challenges faced by their children. It was one of the most popular classes we held. Let me be clear; most parents want to be successful parents and want their children to succeed. And most parents could benefit from a better understanding of how to be more effective in their role. And if some parents request help, as the African American parents in Riverside did, we should try to help them.

It is particularly important to help low-income parents under-stand what they can do to help their children be more effective in school. They want to help, but they are often overwhelmed by cir-cumstances, and the school can help. Study after study has shown that the home environment is critical to student success. The greatest corollary for SAT scores is parent wealth: the richer the parent, the higher the score. I used to joke that if district leaders wanted to raise its SAT scores, all they needed to do was get their children born into wealthier families. Well, obviously, that is not a plan that will work. This is also a very serious indictment of a class-based system, which we still have in this country. The children we have are born to those they were born to, and we have to work with that. But we can look at what it is that makes children of wealthy parents more successful and give those insights to the parents who are less fortunate. But it is important not to just assume low-income parents have problems. When I was in Princeton, a very wealthy community, we found many children were "psychologically abandoned" by parents who were too busy with their careers and lives to help their children. Childrearing in America is a major issue, and to the extent that schools can better support more effective childrearing, we should.

But social class still underpins many educational issues. There have been studies conducted on parent language—how many words an hour they speak to their children. One study by Betty Hart and Todd Risley (2003) at the University of Kansas showed that, on average, professional parents speak 2,000 words an hour to their children while working-class parents speak 1,300 words an hour, and low-income mothers speak 600 words an hour. This means that by age three, children of professional parents have a vocabulary 50% greater than working-class children and 200% greater than low-income children. Other studies have looked at the kinds of words parents speak to children. Are they reprimanding or encouraging? Again, middle-class parents significantly use more encouraging language while lower-income parents use more reprimand. Because children from middle- and upper-middle-class homes have many more words spoken to them than those of low-income homes and they received many more encouraging words than reprimands than low-income children, it should be no surprise that this impacts student achievement.

Giving low-income parents this awareness and showing what they can do to help their children could have a significant impact on later achievement. A small change could come from them taking their children to the supermarket, and then, instead of telling the children to keep their hands off everything, the parent talks to them about what they are doing and ask the children questions about what they are seeing. This will build language and vocabulary. We cannot take children who have had four or five years of limited language development and expect that they will be successful in school. But we can begin to intervene in those first five years to start to change the arc of their lives by helping their parents do a great job as the child's first teacher. But to do so requires that schools rethink their organization and philosophy to make certain that parents are central in that thinking.

Certainly, the issue of early childhood education is also central to all this. Many of the developed countries, as a matter of course, enter children in formal schooling at age three and provide quality day care even earlier. In America, our day care is a patchwork of solutions. Some good and some pretty awful—and that is just for those who can access day care. The research that grew out of the Perry Preschool program (Schweinhart, 1994), years ago, showing that students who have Headstart programs benefit for years should be no surprise, but it hasn't had much impact on policy at the state or national level. The point here is that giving children experiences that stimulate them and offering them opportunities for vocabulary development that affirms them would have tremendous payoffs for the country.

But engaging parents and offering early learning experiences is not enough. Schools must find ways of getting the whole community involved in the education of children. In most communities, only about 30% of the population has children in school. The rest have either already raised their children or do not have children. This is a critical issue for schools as they try to pass budget or bond votes—you are talking to people who feel they do not have a dog in the fight and who care much less about what happens to children. The attitude is either "it's not my problem" or "I raised my kids; now, it is someone else's problem." So if for no other reason than the most practical, schools must reach out to the community. But the community can play a much larger part—they can help educate children.

With the graying of the baby boomers, there are increasing numbers of people who are retired and underutilized. They have much to offer. The creation of volunteer and tutoring programs can draw on this valuable resource. Study after study shows that if a child feels connected, they do better. Being connected to a caring adult can make all the difference for many children. A core human need is having a sense of purpose. Making it easy for members of the community to contribute to the future of children is a very powerful purpose, and it gives the children, many of whom come from homes where the support is often not available, the scaffolding to become stronger.

It is also clear that we live in a society that segregates our population by age. Most nonparenting adults have little contact with children. Because of our mobile society, most children today do not live near their grandparents and have little contact with older people. Finding ways to bring adults into schools helps offset this. Schools, rather than trying to keep nonparents out, should find ways of bringing them into the building. In the district I led in Princeton, New Jersey, we opened our cafeteria to the adults in the community. It helped our food service bottom line, it helped some of the elderly in the community who were on fixed incomes (and made them like us a lot more), and it put students in contact with a different generation. We also opened classes that had excess seats to adults. I once walked into a class that was studying World War II that had a "community student" there who had actually fought in World War II. Imagine the lively discussion I was able to hear—talk about living history! There are hundreds of ways to connect the schools to the community. We are limited only by our imagination and our courage to step out of the commonly accepted ideas of what schools should look like.

One of the key ways of involving community with school is through the creation of *community schools*. These are places where not only courses are offered to the community but also the resources of the community are brought in to serve the children. A school I had in Riverside, California, set up a clinic where doctors and dentists had regular visits to service children at the school, but they also serviced the low-income parents who needed help. The school also had resident social workers from some of the community organizations who found it much easier to gain access to students and their families by being in the school than in trying to get them to come to their locations. We even had a branch of the welfare office there so parents didn't have to go downtown to get service. New York City has had a longstanding relationship with the Children's Aid Society, which has done great work in bringing support resources from the community into the school in a number of settings. The point is that there are many ways to get this done, but it has to start with a sense of openness from the school to get things moving.

One of the major ways schools can work with the community is in the area of afterschool activities. Not only should school facilities be made available to the community but also the community can support the needs of the school in the afterschool area. After we were able to pass a bond in Princeton to upgrade our athletic facilities, we welcomed the community to use them when they were not being used by students. We had people playing ball on our fields and jogging on our track. It made the next bond a lot easier to pass because people saw they benefited too. But again, in the afterschool area, there are nonprofits that provide the care. Giving them access to facilities opens up possibilities for them and makes it easier on the children. You can also provide more enrichment activities by inviting the community to share their expertise with students. We had mothers who had no formal education but who could cook or do crafts leading classes on those things they were good at. In the low-income areas, this had the added bonus of letting the parents and students know that we valued what they and their families were bringing to the school.

You can also benefit the staff with more community involvement. In Princeton, we had an annual symposium where we invited members of the community who were doing interesting work to share it with our staff. Because we were very rich in community intellectual capital, we had professors and researchers to draw from. A community less endowed might be able to use small-business people or farmers to bring insight to the staff. The point here is that the staff learns something and the community walks away with a deeper appreciation of its teaching force. It is a win-win.

To do any of this village-raising requires a new attitude from school leaders. I have often suggested that we should stop talking about superintendents of schools or principals of schools and start talking about superintendents or principals of *learning*. It is not about the place as an isolated venue but about the processes and the relationships. We have to see leaders worry less about the killer Bs of leadership—buildings, buses, books, bonds, budgets— and begin to be become master of the Cs—communication, community building, collaboration, and connection. It is about understanding that learning is a 24/7 proposition. The school plays an important role as facilitator, but to truly make a difference in the lives of children, the whole 360 degrees of their existence must be taken into consideration. Getting children ready for school means starting to think about what needs to happen at the prenatal level and how the schools might have an impact on that. It means finding ways to see that their health needs are met while they are toddlers and what the school can do to facilitate that. It means finding ways to help parents parent effectively. It means finding ways of bringing the school and community together to make a difference in the lives of children. We know much of the child's critical learning takes place well before they get to school. We must find ways of intervening in those years so that positive results can ensue. And we know that about 90% of a child's life is spent outside of school, and we have to create ways of working with parents and the community to see that those hours are not wasted. This is raising the village and putting parachutes on the children, so when they fall down, they won't get hurt.

CHAPTER NINE

Getting Schools Ready for Kids

Treat people like zombies and they'll behave like zombies. But treat them as intelligent and they'll respond intelligently.

—Hans Monderman

In some ways, transforming education means we have to turn everything upside down and inside out. What we are doing and the way we are doing it must change. That seems like a daunting task, which is one of the reasons we haven't really tried to make a major transformation. But more basic is the difficulty of change. People want better schools, but they don't want them different, and yet to be better, they must be different. We all have a mental model of what schools look like that comes from our childhood. If we create something foreign to that model, we get very uncomfortable. We think school should be a place where there is a classroom, kids in desks, and a teacher up front talking and asking kids to take out their textbooks. This image is so ingrained because it has pretty much typified the way schools have been for a very long time. But we can't afford for schools to be places where children must fit. They need to be places that fit to kids and that will require a very different model of education than the traditional one we all remember.

On the other hand, making the transition to schools that are ready for kids can be rather simple. We need to make them places kids want to be. We need to make them places that are welcoming and where the work is meaningful. Much of this will not be a change in form so much as it is a change in substance. We have to worry less about the answers children provide and more about teaching the kinds of questions that they need to ask. And we must be prepared to handle those questions with openness and honesty.

When school people gather, they talk about the "helicopter" parents who are always hovering just above things, ready to swarm in and storm the beachheads at the slightest threat to their children. We have seen that played in all sorts of ways over the past few years, from the irate parent who sues the school over the least issue to the rise of homeschooling, which is an extreme where parents won't entrust their children to the system. The controversy over the President's speech to schoolchildren in 2009 was but another manifestation. Some parents who disagreed with the President politically were so afraid of what the president might say that they kept their children home to protect them from him. Much of this grows out of the values culture clash, but some of it is just out of fear. Couple this with a very prescriptive educational model being passed down by federal and state officials, and the schools feel pretty hemmed in. It is no wonder that we have not seen the kinds of transformative change that is required to remake the system.

So what would it take to create schools kids want to go to? So much of the solution is to make schools look like much of the rest of their lives. Children today are exposed to all sorts of sophisticated technology from Wii to texting. Yet little of that is seen in schools. Which is more engaging, "Turn you books to page 42," or "Let's turn on our simulations?" Another change that has been tried on a more limited scale, as was earlier suggested, is taking kids into the community to do real work. If we could give children experiences in the real world, which has consequences, rather than giving those experiences in the unreal world of the school, which has little consequence, it would make a huge difference.

Further, little things can mean a lot. For example, Cibola High School in Yuma, Arizona, is typical of many high schools along the southern border of the United States. It suffered from low achievement and a large dropout problem. Most of its students were on free or reduced lunch, which is the bellwether for the impact that poverty has on education. The higher the percentage of kids who cannot afford to even buy their lunch, the greater the chance they are going to lag in class. Cibola set out to change this. And what they did was remarkable and simple. The school started working on the issue of "faith." It wasn't the kind preached about on Sunday morning. It was the kind that should permeate any school and already does schools with low numbers of kids in poverty. It is the faith that the student can make it and, in doing so, make a difference. Instead of talking about lowering their dropout rate, they focused on raising their college admission rate. The coin of the realm in that school became college preparation. Rather than letting the kids believe they were being prepared for low-end jobs and a lower future, the teachers and administrators put a full-court press on getting them ready for college. The results are remarkable. Even though they didn't emphasize lowering the dropout rate, they have lowered it significantly. And the graduates now go to college in numbers exceeding 90%. What was the difference? As one student I heard describe it, "They care about me." That sense of caring permeates the school. The philosophy of the school as worked out by the staff is to create a school that runs like a successful family. They see their major focus as saying yes to kids.

A similar national program is Community in Schools (CIS), the most successful dropout prevention program in America. What is their secret? They merely connect the resources that are already in the community with the needs of students. And they try to make sure that every student knows they have a caring adult who wants to see them succeed. The alumni of CIS have not only stayed in school but also have gone on to success in the military, in education, and in business. Their story is one of turning kids around, and they started with that same sense of caring exhibited at Cibola.

Another way of making the change is asking ourselves this simple question—is education instrumental or fundamental? Much of the current focus on education grows out of a belief that it is an instrument to something else: a better job, a more successful economy, national security. But again, for centuries, the purpose of education was much simpler—to create an educated person who could live a full, productive, and contributing life. Education was fundamental. Until we get the answer to this question straight, we are going to continue to get results that do not please us. If education is simply to help the student get a job, what happens in an economic downturn where there are not enough jobs available? If it is simply to make our corporations more successful, then why would we be emphasizing rote responses rather than higher-order thinking skills? Education has to be seen as important for itself. I would like to think I am an educated person, and as such, I am a seeker. I look for books and articles that broaden my perspective and stretch me in new directions. My reading is eclectic and my interests diverse. And I try to spend as much of my time listening as I do talking. I sometimes learn something by talking, but I almost always learn something by listening to others—particularly when it is about something that I am unfamiliar with.

Educational thinker Phil Schlecty opined at a conference I attended that school is a place where the relatively young go to watch the relatively old work. He goes on to suggest that if you want to know who is working in school look at the energy levels at the end of the day. The kids run out, and the teachers stumble out. Again, one of the simple ways of turning things upside down is to make certain that the kids are doing the work. If the teacher is in front of the class talking all day, then the kids are just along for the ride. The classroom needs to be structured like the one I saw in New Zealand, with everyone working all the time.

And we have to focus on *how* we teach more than *what* we teach. With the rapid changes brought about by technology, information is at the child's fingertips. Why would we expend precious class time dealing with facts when they are so easily accessible? We need to spend time on helping students separate the wheat of wisdom from the chaff of useless information. We have to help them sort through what they see and hear and find ways of learning what is true and what is propaganda. This requires them to compare and contrast ideas. They have to dig deeper and look more broadly.

When I was a fledgling teacher, I created a project built around the newspaper. I taught all the classes from the paper. We found our math in the numbers in the paper. Our social studies came out of the news. We did our language arts through extensive reading, and we created our own newspaper. The most significant part of the project was that we didn't create one newspaper, but several. I divided them into several groups. Each was their own paper. To create the news, each group had to "perform" a news event of their creation, which the other groups reported and published. Aside from the creativity involved in creating their little plays, the real learning came not from the performance or the writing. It came when they discovered how differently they had reported the same events. That led to many discussions of bias and how to get past it. We looked at the New York Times and the New York Post to see how they had reported the same event. If nothing else, the students walked away from that experience with a suspended belief in the "truth" they saw and heard around them from the media and with a sense of their responsibility to look past the surface of things to really understand.

Education has to be about more than the acquiring of knowledge. It has to be about the creation of knowledge. Students need to learn to value their ideas and to trust their instincts about what is right or wrong. The root of education is its original meaning in the Latin, "educare"—to bring forth. The way we do school has to be built around drawing forth what students already know and then helping them fill the gaps in their understanding. They have to not only answer the questions but also they need to question the answers. That means they have to have confidence in their thoughts coupled with a healthy skepticism of their beliefs.

In the early 1980s, I was superintendent in the Princeton Regional Schools. I wanted to push toward the future, and I convened a very high-powered committee to look at the future and recommend what we should be doing in the schools about it. This was a form of long-range planning but with a twist. The people I was able to bring together were very atypical for most communities: the vice president of the college board, several other corporate vice presidents, including one whose title was Vice President for the Future. One of the key members was Mike Mahoney, who was a professor of the history of science at Princeton University. He was an unusually broad thinker and a gifted writer. He ended up drafting the committee's work, which took them about two years to complete. They were very prescient predicting, much of what we are even seeing today around the issue of cultural values, technology, and intercultural imperatives.

But the core of their work was around the educational objectives we needed to pursue as a district. They championed the concept of *functional literacy*, which was much broader than most definitions of literacy, even as we understand it today. They meant more than reading, writing, and arithmetic. They saw these as minimal. They felt real literacy had to prepare students for active, comprehending participation in our modern, complex, high-technology, managerial, bureaucratic society. Students needed to have an understanding of how society works, how the economy is structured, how political decisions are reached, and how values are established, and they also need to understand the nature and function of law and the role of individuals and groups of various sizes in maintaining society and fostering its growth. In essence, they saw functional literacy as knowing enough about one's society to feel at home in it.

They laid out three broad objectives. The first was that *students should learn to think and to learn.* This included getting to the point where they were aware of how people think and learn. This meant they needed to acquire access to a variety of ways to think—the abstract formal reasoning of mathematics, the intuitive patterns of thought in the arts, the empirical and inductive methods of scientific investigation, the insights of the humanities, the statistical inquiries of social science, and the concrete problem solving of technology. They pointed out each of these are a way of inquiring about the world and our experience in it. Each inhabits its own realm but overlaps sometimes with other realms. Each has its own form of creativity, which they described as fluency, flexibility, and originality of thought. They pointed out that students need to know the kinds of questions they are trying to answer, so they could use the right kind of process to answer it. In a blazing prediction of the foibles of the current reform agenda, the committee suggested that quantification isn't always appropriate; some matters are not settled by counting. Always, students need to know that many questions have different answers. Students need to know more about the kinds of assertions being made; for example, a statistical statement about smoking and cancer or television and violence presupposes a relationship between cause and effect that is different from the laws of physics.

The second broad objective is that *children need to learn to communicate.* This includes expressing thoughts clearly and concisely in writing or verbally and being able to read and listen sympathetically yet critically. They should also be familiar with various non-verbal modes such as signs, symbols, gestures, music, and the plastic arts. This will allow them to understand the complex ways humans signal their feelings and intentions to one another.

The third imperative called for is that *children need to learn to cooperate*. They need to learn to work together in a multivalued, complex, interdependent society. They need to be able to participate with understanding in the common enterprise of a civilized culture. This includes knowing how society is structured and how you gain access to power. They also need to understand that with a sense of control also comes a sense of responsibility.

The committee went on to suggest that each of the objectives were made of four components: (1) information, (2) skills, (3) appreciation, and (4) attitudes. In essence, what they were saying is that once students mastered the objectives, there would be things they know, things they know how to do, judgments they can make, and traits that they will have acquired. The fourth objective combined the first three but was higher than they were—it was that children should learn to make reasoned and well-informed decisions on which individually and socially responsible actions can be based and by which they will be generated.

The committee understood that the real change in school would come with the appreciation and attitudes and that these would not come from textbooks but from the teachers. For example, teachers sometimes needed to pause in the midst of a lesson to reflect on the elegance of an idea and to let students think about it. They needed to let students have the pleasure of discovering concepts for themselves. They need to create situations where students have to solve problems for themselves but that require collaboration with others.

Once this visionary and challenging report was created, it was left to the administration to figure out how to make it happen. A modest change we made was in the high school physical education (PE) curriculum. At that point, the program was moribund and an object of great criticism. The teachers were not very energized, and the students did everything possible to avoid the deadly days of volleyball and kickball. We introduced Project Adventure, a program created in Massachusetts. It was a ropes challenge course where students had to face individual and group challenges involving jumping from poles to swings, maneuvering through an obstacle course, or getting a group over an eight-foot high wall. It incorporated many of the concepts in the plan—challenge, problem solving, collaboration, and facing the unknown with courage. It became incredibly popular with students, many of whom took PE as an elective just so they could do the program again, and it reenergized the faculty. They would give up their planning period to go out and help their colleagues on the course.

As an administration, we decided to focus on classroom questions as the centerpiece of our supervision and evaluation process. We looked at the kinds of questions teachers asked, the wait time they gave for answers, and the spread of student involvement. We found that most of the questions when we started were low-level response questions, the wait time was less than the time research indicates is necessary to engage the mind, and that about only 20% of the class ever got to answer questions, leaving the rest to observe. With work, we got teachers asking higher-level questions that led to the kinds of thinking suggested in the plan, we got them to wait longer between questions and supplying the answer so real thinking could occur, and we had them distributing the questions more broadly to the class. The real breakthrough came when we started to examine how teachers fielded questions from students. We found that whenever a divergent question was asked by students, teachers tended to squelch them. So it appeared we were going to develop creative, divergent thinking by stamping it out whenever it arose! This was the biggest insight we took from our efforts and the one that most helped the teachers change their way of teaching. As a divergent thinker myself, I wished my teachers had been offered this insight when I was a student.

The ways we teach kids, the kinds of assumptions we make about the purposes of education, and our assumptions about how students learn tend to color and impact the whole way we educate. My friend Paul Heckman, when he was working on the project in Tucson, used to spend a couple hours a week with the teachers asking about their work. One time, he was working with the kindergarten teachers who explained that they were about to embark on a six-week project to teach their students their colors.

"Why are you doing that?" asked Paul.

"Well, you know these are low-income kids, and they come to school not knowing their colors," one of the teachers explained.

"Oh, I see," Paul replied. "You mean they can't tell the difference between this red piece of paper and the blue and green piece?"

"Oh no. They could do that."

"Then you mean they can't tell you that the red piece of paper is the same color as the fire engine in the play corner?"

"No, they can do that."

"Okay, I think I get it. You are saying they don't know that the red piece of paper is the same color as something that is red at home but that they can't see right now?"

"Oh, no, they can do that."

Paul looked at the teachers and kind of scratched his head. "I don't get it. It seems to me they have the concept of color down pretty good. I don't understand what you are going to teach."

One of the teachers said, "Well—the words. They don't know the words."

Paul looked at the teachers and said, "You are going to take six weeks to teach the students labels to put on what they already know. Aren't you really teaching them they must be really stupid to take six weeks to learn something that you should be able to teach them in a few days?"

As the teachers thought about it, they realized he was right, and they modified their plans.

When I was a graduate student at Harvard, I had a professor who told a group of us that he couldn't teach us anything but labels to put on what we already know. It seems to me that when we can approach education with the same respect for low-income students as we reserve for graduate students, then we will be getting someplace. Students know so much more than schools assume. We just haven't found ways to connect their knowing to the broader world that they will need to navigate.

At its core, getting schools ready for kids is really about fitting the schools to the students, not trying to fit the students to the school. It is about looking at all the ways we learn and think and creating programs that help facilitate that. It is about valuing children and what they bring to the table. And it is about personalizing their education so they learn what they need, not what we think they need.

Getting schools ready for kids has to be about changing the mindsets we bring to the table. We have to lose the "mind forged manacles" we bring to how we see schools and be prepared to change their structure, the curriculum, and most important, how we teach kids. That seems, to me, to be at the center of having a possibility of helping kids reach their dreams. It comes from the faith of the teachers at Cibola and the deep understanding of what is needed expressed in the planning report developed in Princeton. And most of all, it comes from the deep belief in what children already know and value, they bring with them, which my friend Paul Heckman has.

CHAPTER TEN

Getting the Words and Symbols Right

What we got here is a failure to communicate.

—Warden in *Cool Hand Luke*

One of my favorite old movies is *Cool Hand Luke* starring Paul Newman. In the movie, Luke is jailed for cutting off the tops of parking meters. He wasn't stealing the money; like a lot our children who act out in school, he was just staving off boredom. He told the judge it was just something to do. Once he is sent to a prison work camp somewhere in the Deep South, his behavior doesn't really change. His rebellious attitude soon puts him at odds with the warden. After sending him several times to spend a night in "the box," a very small building so cramped you couldn't lay down, and seeing no improvement in Luke's behavior, the warden in total exasperation utters, "What we got here is failure to communicate."

From the time we were born, we struggle with the challenge of communication. We mostly seem to be talking past one another. Parents and children tend to miscommunicate, which makes the job of raising children harder than it already is. Men and women have trouble being clear to one another. This creates all sorts of problems in the workplace (not to mention in the family room at home). Different regions communicate differently, which creates problems for school leaders who move from state to state. All this failure to communicate creates issues for schools and makes it more difficult for schools to work with constituents. And teaching students how to effectively communicate is at the center of what schools must do for students.

Parents talk incessantly to their children or more accurately *at* their children in many cases. What children mostly hear is "Blah, blah, blah. Blah blah." As I pointed out in the last chapter, studies have found that depending on social class, parents talk differently to their children. Low-income parents talk less, using about 20% of the words middle-class parents use. Many of the phrases they use are based on punishment, rewards, or directions. Middle-class parents talk much more to their children and use many more encouraging phrases. The upshot is that, often, low-income children are sur-rounded by messages of criticism, and middle-class children hear more messages of possibility. It isn't that one group loves their children more; it is just that they learned to communicate differently. It is no wonder one group tends to struggle in school much more than the other. But at the end of the day, children of any social class pay less attention to what parents have to say than most parents would like. And most children feel their parents don't listen to them and "just don't understand," to borrow the words of a Will Smith song (Jazzy Jeff & Fresh Prince, 1998). It often seems that children and parents are speaking a different language.

As we grow up, things don't seem to get better. Certainly, the battle of the sexes is, at its core, language driven. There has been a whole cottage industry devoted to this. Bestselling books, plays, and movies have taken on the communication differences between men and women. Men drive themselves crazy trying to figure out what women want, and women wonder what in the world men are thinking. After a lifetime of research, I can answer both of these questions. It boils down to the fact that women don't know what they want. Or more precisely, it depends on when you ask them. Sometimes they want one thing, at other times something else.

And for men, the answer is even easier. What are they thinking? Not much. Men don't tend to analyze what is happening in their lives. Sometimes they just want to go in their "caves" until the fog lifts or the bear decides to leave. When women try to get past the "man silence" that confronts them, men don't like it. Women are complex and layered. For that reason, men can't read them. Women think men are just as complex and layered, and they assume there is more going on behind the curtain. Men aren't, and it isn't. This leads to the confusion.

It would appear that much of the confusion between sexes boils down to communication style and needs. Women need to talk it out, and for men, silence is golden. The less talk the better. It has been my observation that these gender styles carry over into the workplace. Women put a premium on process, and men put it on outcomes. Neither is particularly right nor wrong. Both are necessary for positive results. You can see how this makes it difficult for people working in schools and for how schools communicate with the public. Our communication has to be much more sophisticated and should take the audience into consideration.

The communication issue is also regional. I have lived in the north, south, east, and west. I even spent some time in Middle America. Every region has its way of communicating. Midwesterners are plain spoken, open, and friendly. West-coast folks tend to be up on the latest pop psychology, and its phrases sprinkle their language. I grew up in the south, which uses a lot of what I call "social lubrication" in communication. In other words, a Southerner will often avoid saying things directly. If a Southerner says, "He did real good, considering," that really means that he did real good considering his father left the family. Another Southerner gets that immediately. Or they insert "bless her heart" into the discussion; it doesn't really mean bless her heart. It means, "God help her for being so backward." I remember when I moved to the north from the south, I thought everyone was very rude because they were so direct. Nothing had varnish on it. I couldn't believe people talked that way to one another. Every phrase was full of "fighting words." Living in the north, I discovered that Northerners think Southerners are so disingenuous. "Why don't they just say what they mean instead of beating around the bush?" Or they think they are just too stupid to spit it out. No wonder we fought a war between the two regions, and no wonder educators who move from one region to another sometimes get into trouble for communicating inappropriately.

We are all familiar with the way countries have difficulty communicating. The fact that we have different languages is just part of it. Language is a window to the culture. We have all heard that Eskimos have many different words for snow because it is such a central part of their culture, but the reality is that there is also a difference in their language that leads to this as well. I have heard about cultures that have no word for "time" or for "want." That would dramatically shape your worldview. Rushing to attain worldly goods would have no basis for understanding in that culture. Trying to force more industriousness on them would have no meaning. We tend to view others through our lens and our understanding. I remember reading a piece during the Iranian hostage crisis in the early 1980s. Our folks in Washington were trying to figure out what the Ayatollah Khomeini wanted when he said that to resolve things he wanted the Shah's head on a platter. People were staying up late at the CIA trying to figure out what that meant. What was his metaphor? Turns out, it wasn't a metaphor. He really did want the Shah's head on a platter.

This difference in communication between countries has led to the use of a very specific way of talking. It is called *diplomatic language*. This is used to reduce friction between countries and reduce tension. It is supposed to smooth over differences, but often, it sounds like nothing is being said. It is so soft that it doesn't convey some of the deeper issues. And because the world still is rift with war, we see there is a limit to the effectiveness of this style of communication. I have noticed that schools often use their own form of diplomatic language. We often don't really tell a parent what is happening with their child because we wrap our talk in such euphemisms and jargon that the parent has no clue what is really happening to their child. Educational jargon and "educationese" does more to block our connection with parents and the community than almost anything else we do. We have known this for a long time, and yet we continue to build word fortresses around our schools and wonder why the hordes are attacking.

Lately, technology has given us whole new ways to miscommunicate with one another. Most organizations now use e-mail and millions of us use it for private communication. This is supposed to enhance communication. Often, it has the opposite effect. E-mail messages tend to be brief, which leads them to sound curt. There is rarely context offered, and they are written quickly, so they lack nuance. This often leads to misunderstanding, hurt feelings, and conflict that previously didn't exist. Text messaging is even worse, not to mention it is creating a whole new language that is so stripped of meaning, it even leaves out most of the letters of the words. And the new sensation "tweeting" is even less effusive. Further, all these forms lack a visual and tonal cue, which leads to even further communication issues. It has been observed that about 70% of all communication is nonverbal. What happens to a society when it relies simply on verbal messages for communication? And how do we help students understand tone, context, and body language when they are exposed to so little of it?

The challenge for education in all this is immense. Not only are we failing to tackle these issues but also much of what we are doing is making it worse. It isn't just dealing with the question of "Why Johnny can't read" (a popular topic after Sputnik) but why he cannot write, cannot express himself clearly in spoken language, can't listen, and can't read social signals. Language is both expressive and receptive. A great school environment teaches students not just the basics of reading and writing but also the basics of speaking and listening. And listening isn't just hearing but understanding the meaning behind the meaning. Much of it has to do with context and nuance.

When I was superintendent in Princeton, I came to understand that it was a community of scholars. Language was important, so I found that when I spoke at meetings, I had to consider the nuance and connotation of each word. A slight slip and I had trouble on my hands. When I moved to Tucson, I continued to parse my words carefully. I found very quickly that my subtlety was sailing right over people's heads and flying off into the desert night. They expected straight, blunt talk. They didn't like rounded phrases; they wanted things as sharp and stark as the desert landscape. I realized that in the desert, nothing is subtle. Sunsets are vivid. Storms, when they happen, are spectacular. When it gets hot, it gets *hot*! People communicated the same way. There is nothing in superintendent school (or any other for that matter) that teaches this kind of thing. And there is no reason that the communications skills we teach kids shouldn't be much broader than we are currently providing. The ability to communicate in a subtle and sophisticated way sets us apart from other species. We should be doing much more to capitalize on our abilities by teaching our children much more about all aspects of communication.

And we have to start with improving communication by doing a much better job of communicating to our communities. Over the last few years, I have been involved in trying to contact school leaders in their office by phone. In one case, while I was still head of the American Association of School Administrators (AASA), we decided to use a robot calling system to invite people to our national conference. The message was to be sent by computer to the office of the superintendent. It was decided the calls would go out at midnight so they weren't misdirected. A not very funny thing happened on our way to efficiency. It seems that a number of the contact numbers we had were not office numbers but *home* numbers. You can imagine how happy superintendents were to be getting a call at midnight on their home phone with my friendly voice inviting them to Tampa. You can imagine the fun they had trying to explain to their spouses why they were getting a call at midnight! What kind of a nutcase would call at midnight? The kind of nutcase who relied too much on technology. We had to go back to the drawing board.

So learning from our mistake, we had staff call the office so it was human to human. Guess what? We found it is virtually impossible to get a human when you call most school districts. It was about as satisfying as calling the Department of Motor Vehicles. First of all, superintendents have great gatekeepers. So if you did get a human, you weren't about to get to talk to the superintendent. They wouldn't let Moses through to speak to the superintendent even if he had the message written on two tablets of stone. Most of the time, you don't get a human. You get a recording. Many school systems have these recorded systems where the caller gets a recording telling them what number to push to get to the right person. However, we found that most of the time it doesn't work that way. We were just as likely to get to the bus barn as the superintendent's office. Now, I could have had my computer talk to their answering system, but that is not the best way to develop understanding. An over reliance on technology is the worst way to improve human communication. In our rush to be efficient, we have lost the human side of the proposition, and when that is lost, communication is lost.

One of the biggest detriments to communication is the language we use. Educators are often accused of using educationese instead of English. We use big or esoteric words when smaller, more universal ones will do much better to get our point across. We need to watch our words and reduce the acronyms. Most educators don't even know what all the alphabet soup means. Why do we assume our constituency will get it? I have always wondered if we talk that way to sound more important or to create a distance with parents and community. Well, it doesn't make us sound more important. It makes us sound pretentious. But it does create a distance for us. For education to be effective, we must involve parents and the broader community. We can't do that by making it harder for them to contact us, and when they do, they shouldn't have to feel like they need a translator to converse with us.

Although communicating is hard, God gave us two ears and one tongue for a reason. It allows us to listen more than we talk. In our work, we tend to get so wrapped up in talking (and speaking in "tongues") that we fail to listen. Or we listen only long enough to get what we think the other person is saying, and then we barge in with our explanation or excuse. It is important for all of us but particularly for educators to listen for what is behind the words. I attended a board meeting once where they were having a lot of controversy over library books. It boiled down to the classic liberal/conservative split of who has a right to say what is taught. As I listened to the parents who wanted the books banned, I realized that what they really wanted was for their children to be safe. It is vital that educators listen for the "meta" messages—those messages behind the words of parents and the community, and it is crucial that educators watch for the real messages they might be sending.

Yogi Berra once said, "You can observe a lot just by watching." I would also suggest you can hear a lot just by listening. That is not a bad place to start in overcoming our failure to communicate.

CHAPTER ELEVEN

Horse Whispering

*Harnessing Technology
to Enhance Learning*

Computers are useless. They can only give you answers.

—Pablo Picasso

There is nothing with more potential for improving education and more misunderstood than technology. We haven't yet fully realized what technology can do *for* education or what it has done *to* education. There is great potential and tremendous confusion. It should be a major tool for educators, but we have to know how to use the tool and how to make it work in conjunction with what we want to do for students. It reminds me of the time I met Monty Roberts (1996) known as the "Horse Whisperer." Monty's fame came from his ability to break wild horses and to train them, not by using the old methods of riding the horse until he breaks it down and into submission. Monty's technique was what he called "meeting up" with the horse. He approached it with the respect of one creature meeting another on equal ground. He would talk gently to it, and through kindness and perseverance, he would persuade it to do his bidding. This is a wonderful metaphor for how we should work with children, but it is also a wonderful metaphor for how we should be using technology in schools. We have to find ways of "meeting up" with the technology and not trying to force it in ways that will not work.

Schools have always been bombarded with new technology, promising to revolutionize the learning process. First, it was radio, which made no dent in education, and then it was television, which was used sporadically. We were promised the wonders of educational television, but it was rarely used with effect. Some districts had their own stations for producing and broadcasting programs into schools. Although this was a good way to spread information, its lack of interaction limited its effectiveness with students. I remember how people thought the overhead projector was going to change things. It did help teachers because they could write and display information to the entire class without turning their backs to the kids (always a dangerous act!), but nothing hit education like the advent of the computer. It was going to change everything. But something happened on the way to the revolution. Since the early 1980s, when computers were first being introduced to students, the public's confidence in education has slipped, and schools are viewed as being failures in producing the kinds of learners needed in the information age. It is almost as if the more we use computers, the less confidence the public has in our overall product or even how we are preparing children for a technological future. Although no one blames the computers for this, it is clear their introduction failed to stem the tide of perceived mediocrity.

I believe that, up to this point, we have failed to use technology properly. Like the old bronco breakers, we have tried to use the technology as a power tool on the kids. By throwing enough technology at them, we thought somehow it would change things. Not enough thinking has been applied to what we might do differently and how technology might get us there. It is time we started "whispering" to the kids by using the tools we have available instead of forcing the technology into classrooms without thinking enough about how it could make education exciting and meaningful.

When computers first came on the scene, they were seen as ways to drill students on basic skills or to teach them programming so that they could work in high-tech jobs later on. Then things like Bank Street Writer and Logo were introduced, which allowed children to write in a word processing format or to develop simple programs directing a robot around the room. Because computers were very expensive and few staff knew how to use them, they were mostly put into labs (having usually been purchased with federal money), and those became educational black holes where children's creativity went to die. Computer labs were occasionally used to give students a learning tool. Much more often, they were places for computer-assisted instruction, fondly referred to by many educators as "drill and kill." Students sat in front of the machine, responding to questions and commands. If they got it right, they moved onto the next question. If they got it wrong, they were given a short makeup lesson and then asked another question. We had finally found a more expensive and complex way to kill student's interest in learning.

Little concern was given to the hidden curriculum behind this method. It was simply that the machines knew more than the student and that learning was a stimulus-response system. Not too surprising, despite sizable investments in technology, few gains were seen in learning. Of course, one of the biggest reasons for this was that students had such limited access to and time with a computer; it would have been hard to make much progress. Going to a lab for an hour or two a week will not generate much improvement, no matter how good the program might be. The simple answer to the question of why we haven't seen more impact from technology is that we haven't really tried it.

As the superintendent of the Princeton Regional Schools, at the dawn of computers in schools, we looked at this new world and made an interesting decision. I was helped in this by my assistant superintendent, Jamie McKenzie, who was very visionary when it came to the classroom use of technology. We were fortunate that learning basic skills was not an issue for the vast majority of our children, so investment in "learning labs," as they were called in those days, made no sense. But more important, we knew (and if we forgot the parents reminded us) that we were educating children who would someday take their place as "masters of the universe" or at least professors and CEOs. Sitting in front of a machine and being told what to do isn't the best route to learning how to run things. We felt the kids should be telling the machines what to do. That meant they had to be using the computer as a learning tool. We made certain that there were computers in every classroom and that the kids would be expected to do writing and researching with them. We used Bank Street Writer with our younger kids and other word processing programs with the middle and high school students. We made sure every middle school student learned keyboarding skills. We teamed up with a local corporation that was in the information business, and we developed one of the first research curriculums using the Internet. We never tried to sell the cost of the computers to our community as an investment in test scores. We simply pointed out that in the world of the future everyone would be using technology as a basic tool and so should our children. Rather than having to fight for enough money, we often had to fight off parents who wanted us to move faster and to do and buy more.

One of the things we learned early on was that there were many unintended consequences of what we were doing. For example, we found we had to modify some of our language curriculum because the kids needed much more precision in their vocabularies if they were going to do effective searches on the Internet. We also realized early on that the Internet afforded a much better way for students to cheat and plagiarize. So we had to get into ethics with them. We also found that we had to work with the kids so they could see that not everything they read online was true. The biggest thing we learned was that the really good learning came about almost accidentally. Teachers were constantly coming to us to tell us something they had discovered with the kids well outside of the planned program. So we built "playing around" into our efforts. We didn't know the potential of what we had, and we would only find it by open exploration. This is probably a good metaphor for learning as well. Some of the best inventions of man came from accidents or mistakes (The sticky note comes to mind.) When it comes to technology, we have to be forgiving of the mistakes and open to the accidents that can lead to breakthroughs in learning.

When I went to Tucson, as superintendent, I was able to lead the passage of a large bond program, a part of which paid for a large investment in technology. Now, it is not smart to use bonds to buy machines that will not live out the life of the bond, but it was the only way we could jump-start the system toward being technologically sound. At that point, we were well behind the curve. I was lucky to have a major technology visionary inside the system, Jesse Rodriguez, who really understood where technology was going and what it could do. Jessie won me over early on when he, as a low-level employee, convinced me that a major mainframe purchase we were about to make would be a huge error. Or as he put it, it would be a great five-million dollar anchor if I just had a boat to use it with. I put him in charge of leading our efforts toward a distributed networking system. As Jesse put it, I was trying to create a site-based district, and I needed to make sure that I didn't keep the brains of the system centralized. Tucson became one of the earliest major organizations, inside or outside of education, to go with distributed networking, and we received lots of national attention because of it, so Jesse had my trust.

One day he came to my office and asked me if I would support an experiment he wanted to try. Because we had agreed no one had ever tried to use technology as an ultimate tool, he wanted to equip one of our middle schools so that every child had a computer and all the teachers would be trained to redo the curriculum so that students used the computers all day as their basic learning tool. Actually, at first, we only equipped half the school because we wanted to research the difference this might make, so half the school was the control group.

Once the Maxwell program was up and running, some interesting things started to happen. Test scores increased significantly for those using the technology. Attendance increased rather dramatically. The group using the technology had an average of 19 days of absence a year, as compared to the others who had 27 days of absence. Discipline referrals dropped markedly. And enrollment increased. How? At that time, Maxwell was a "walk-in school" with no buses. It also served a low-income area, so there was lots of mobility. As we implemented the program, parents made sure their children stayed in school, and if they moved, they transported them to school. The reason was simply; as one of the parents put it, "The kids want to learn." One of the students said, "I want to study. I want to figure this out." What we had unwittingly done was change the climate of the school to one where students were interested and engaged in the learning process in ways they had not been up to that point.

Also, although both Microsoft and Compaq had been involved in education and Compaq was an early supporter of the project,

Jesse was able to show them that the machines and programs they had created for the business world worked with students—even middle schoolers! Up to that point, neither company had seen these products as school related. Representatives from both companies told me later that Jesse had been a big reason they had gotten into education more completely. They could see their products being used with children. The kids didn't know they were using adult products.

The Maxwell project reconstituted the school to allow the kids to become "techno-centric." It gave the kids access to technology in an anytime, anyplace environment. Because the kids had their own computer, they did all their work on it. They took it home. They could access their work from one class in a different class or on the weekends. The school day and the egg-crate design of the school no longer limited them to learning one subject in one room or to the formal hours of the school day. Maxwell became a testing ground for making the kids not only techno-centric but info-centric. It changed the way teachers taught. They developed an integrated curriculum that was accessible at all times for the students.

But more than just being techno- or info-centric, Maxwell also started the process of restructuring the learning process. Historically, school has centered on the teacher, with the student and family as supporting players. We started flipping the pyramid so that students moved to the top, and teachers became a support system along with the home and the other support staff in the school. Kids should be the primary gatherer of knowledge, and then they should be creating information that did not previously exist, like those kids in Olathe who invented their own insulation. School should be a place where invention is a way of life.

One of the challenges with technology is that it keeps developing and becoming more sophisticated with what it can be. That means we have to keep moving and becoming more sophisticated. Now tiny computers have more power than large mainframes did a few years ago. Today, we would never even have to face the decision of mainframe versus distributed. My cell phone has more computing power than the Apollo 11 moon ship. Handheld devices and the phones we use are capable of all sorts of functions. In a few years, we won't need laptops—we'll just need "handtops" to do even more work. Much of that technology already exists. We are just lacking the bandwidth to carry the information. But that will come. The good news is that the kids are capable of handling these changes. They embrace technology as "digital natives," as they have been called, and they are at home in this land that seems so strange to those of us who thought the overhead projector was a big breakthrough.

In the not too distant future, assignments will be on their handhelds, testing will be done on the handhelds, and groups and teams will operate virtually. The school will be as big as the world. In fact, they are already doing a lot of this—outside the school. The fact is the world has passed the schools by. Children have embraced the brave new world of ubiquitous technology. In technology, there are the concepts of a "closed system" and an "open system." Early on, companies tried to keep their systems closed so that you had to buy hardware and software together. That did not work. Openness is the name of the game. Yet schools still act as a closed system, lacking the awareness of what is happening around us. The kids know better. Schools are the lagging indicator of technological advances. Technology doesn't close its doors at 3:00 p.m. or over the summer. Kids are always on. How can we remake our schools so they are always on as well? That is our challenge.

Further, the technology already exists to allow schools to provide an individualized education plan (IEP) for *every* student. Whenever I have mentioned this with school leaders, they have cringed because up to now an IEP was attached to the special education programs for disabled students and had legal consequences. Parents sued schools that failed to deliver on the plans. What I am suggesting is not a system forced on the schools by legal means but a solution for all children.

We don't have to keep dooming children to the Procrustean bed that has only one size. Before the spread of technology, it was virtually impossible for a teacher to take into account every individual learning style, set of strengths and weaknesses and match the curriculum to those. Today, it can and should be done. We can personalize education for every child. I believe, in the near future, schools will be expected, as a matter of course, to develop a personalized educational plan (PEP) for all students that focuses on assets and deficits and charts a learning program unique to their abilities and interests. This is only possible through the breakthroughs available through technology.

If you look at Amazon, UPS, Wal-Mart, FedEx, or even the United States Postal Service, they use technology to track their customers' wants and needs. They know what you bought and suggest other products that might interest you. They know exactly what they have in inventory and know where every package is, wherever it is in the world. If they can do that, shouldn't schools be focusing on getting personalized education on track? If FedEx knows where every package it has accepted is, anytime, anywhere in the world, we should be able to keep track of the learning of a few hundred students in a school.

In five years, handheld devices will be able to do everything a net book can currently do. In 10 years, they will be able to do anything a desktop can do. At some point, schools need to stop outlawing cell phones and start having them used as key learning tools. In the not too distant future, every child will have an avatar that will be a virtual tutor and personal researcher that can gather information from a variety of sources and lay it at the student's feet. They will be a virtual "you" but designed to assist learning. We already have "Second Life," which many adults use that created a virtual you in a parallel virtual world. In the not too distant future, if a student wants to study ancient Rome, they will be taken on a tour of it by their avatar where they will see gladiators in action and the Roman Senate planning and plotting, and they will be able to interact with them. Maybe they will discover how much fun history can be.

The world of gaming is already getting close to this reality. We have seen in gaming that kids will do things repeatedly to get to a different level. It also allows them to play against others in other parts of the world. They can team up and compete with friends from Java and Japan. This drive, persistence, and collaboration would be a welcome addition to most classrooms. The game inventors already know how to capture the children's attention and imagination. We could learn from them.

We can already do some of this, even at a more primitive level. In 1990, in the Maxwell project, the school had the kids measure their runs around the track. How long did it take? How high was their heart rate? How long did it take their heart to return to resting level? Then the kids took this information and put it on Excel spreadsheets. They graphed the results and compared them. They could then measure their progress and see what increased levels of exercise did for them. They would do this kind of work later in the adult work environment. But for them, it was just plain interesting. It appealed to their competitive spirit, and it addressed their individual interests.

Much of the new technological development in the future will be led by the students. Schools should try to stay out of the way of this. Joshua Ramo (2009), in his book *The Age of the Unthinkable*, suggests that in the emerging era of chaos, wealth will be measured not in money and power but in the ability to change and adapt. He suggests that the more users a centralized system has, the closer it comes to exhaustion, but the more users a decentralized system has, the more efficient it becomes because the work can be spread around. This has huge implications for all facets of education but none more than the use of technology. Rather than trying to hold the decisions and the expertise at the adult level, giving the students more ownership and opportunity to contribute will create faster and deeper changes.

No one can accurately predict all the ways technology will be used in the future, in part, because there will be even greater breakthroughs in the future. We do know that the machines we are creating are getting faster and more powerful while they are getting smaller and cheaper. This has tremendous implications for schools because the issue of budgets will be less pervasive. But we cannot predict the future because we cannot know what innovation will come from the consumers—the children. What is clear is technology makes the finding of the Holy Grail of learning—a completely personalized learning experience for each child—not just possible but inevitable. What is also clear is that school people need to give over more power and possibility to the teachers and students. And this will lead to enormous learning possibilities, motivated students, and successful teachers.

CHAPTER TWELVE

The Brain Is a Terrible Thing to Waste

Sometimes I sits and thinks. And sometimes I just sits.

—Attributed to Satchel Paige

Two major breakthroughs allow us to think about education differently from past generations. Technology is the first, and what we have learned about the brain is the second. The last 20 years have presented significant new understanding of how the brain functions, what it can do, and how we can make it more effective. This has tremendous implications for education.

What I find so interesting is that so little of what we know has found its way into practice. There are several reasons for that. The first is the vast gulf between research and practice. This has always existed in education. For example, research has consistently shown that if you retain children in the same grade for a second year because they haven't made sufficient progress, they do worse the second year. Yet the last few years has seen a spate of laws and policies requiring retention and forbidding *social promotion*. Some educators are aware of this research but have been unable to stop the policymakers from doing their worst. I am glad they passed me on without adequate skills when I was in first grade, or I would be the oldest first grader in America!

When it comes to brain research, even most educators are behind the times. We know, for example, that the teenage brain has a different biorhythm than that of younger children. It comes to life later and stays alert later. Yet most school systems start high school earlier than the lower grades on the assumption that because the secondary kids are older, they can be safer waiting for buses in the dark, and they need the time in the afternoon for athletics. A few districts have considered the research and modified their start times. Ken Dragseth, a former National Superintendent of the Year and past superintendent in Edina, Minnesota, an affluent suburb of Minneapolis, understood the research and was brave enough and clever enough to move the school start time later, which more closely matched the start time of the teenage mind. They have seen improved academic performance.

Another thing we know from research is that the wiring in the brain that helps us learn other languages becomes firmer early in a child's life. Yet we wait to teach languages much later in the school experience. Some of the research on this is fascinating. It appears that you do not need to teach a child the entire language at an early age. If you can teach them a couple hundred words, it allows the brain to learn the pattern of the language, which can be built on later. Imagine a school where kindergarten children are exposed to multiple languages throughout the year, and then this is built on as they grow. There is an old joke that asks, "What do you call someone who knows two languages?" The answer is "bilingual." Likewise, "What do you call someone who knows three languages?" The answer, of course, is "trilingual." But if you ask, "What do you call a person who only knows one language?" The answer is "American." This joke is less than funny in a global context. As we are asking our children to compete and succeed in a world of many languages, we are handicapping them with bad policy that is not based on what we know about learning. And this is easily remedied.

There have been many significant breakthroughs in understanding the brain and how it learns. One of the most significant is the work being done in neuroplasticity. This comes from a lot of work that has been done with brains that have been damaged through accident or medical trauma. What the researchers have learned is that not only is the brain wired for certain things but it is also capable of rewiring itself. The implications for education in this are staggering. Although educators have mouthed the notion that "all children can learn" for years, there has been a lot of inaction that tends to undercut this proclamation. In fact, there is a sense that many kids can learn not so much. The advent of IQ testing in the early part of the last century implied that intelligence was fixed and had a lot to do with inheritance. Likewise, the dominance of the bell curve that posited a bell-shaped distribution of intelligence and ability assumes not all of us were intellectually created equal. Neuroplasticity undermines the foundation on which so much of the educational assumptions have been built on.

There is a seminal book out on the issue of europlasticity called *The Brain That Changes Itself* by Norman Doidge (2007). In this book, Doidge points out that our senses have an unexpectedly plastic nature. If one is damaged, another can take over for it. This is the reason that blind people often have acute hearing. Further, it has been found that we see with our brains, not with our eyes. Researchers have found that our eyes see light changes; our brain makes sense of them. There has even been research to show that blind people, rigged with special gloves that allow them to "see" with their hands through skin sensitivity, can see what was previously blind to them. The implications for all this, not just in the medical world but in the educational world, are profound.

A few schools give their students brain exercises. Doidge (2007) cites that the Arrowsmith School in Toronto, Canada, uses brain research extensively in its work with children. Much of this has to do with having students memorize various works. Ironically, what is old is new again. I grew up having to memorize poems and pieces of speeches and then reciting them in class. It appears that if a child has difficulties with brain function, putting them through similar requirements strengthens those areas of weakness. Certain brain deficits can be treated with exercises in rote memorizing. This is not to say that so much of today's education that relies on remembering and regurgitating facts is the way to go. It does mean that thoughtful lessons around specific memorization can be a good thing. The bigger point made by the work at Arrowsmith and a handful of other schools focused on brain-based learning is that you have to exercise the brain just as you do your muscles, and by doing so, you can strengthen it.

The main point here is that many students would benefit if they were given brain-based assessments that would identify their weakened areas and then be given a program to strengthen them. This is more appropriate than simple tutoring that repeats lessons that may not address their weaknesses. If we are going to spend billions of dollars on assessments, perhaps we should start by using those kinds of assessments that might actually lead to better learning. If you couple these brain-based assessments with the power of technology, where lessons could be tailored to the specific needs identified, we might have an educational system that truly proved every child can learn. What we do know for sure is that education matters. Doidge points out that postmortem examinations show that education increases the number of branches among neurons, which leads to an increase in volume and thickness in the brain. It would seem that the old notion that the brain is a muscle that grows with use is more than fantasy.

One of the major researchers in neuroplasticity, Mike Mersenich has actually created a program for schools called Fast ForWord, which is disguised as a game. It has been found that individuals who have had a lifetime of difficulty cognitively can improve dramatically after only about sixty hours of treatment. Fast ForWord uses the fact that our brains are more than computers because, unlike computers, they are constantly adapting. Further, the brain doesn't just learn but it also learns how to learn. This leads to the whole area of metacognition, which is thinking about thinking.

When I was visiting the schools in Singapore, I visited a math classroom. It was Friday. We found that the class had spent the entire week on one problem! This would never happen in an American classroom because of the premium we place on *coverage* of subjects. Teachers feel pressured to cover as much material as possible. Staying on one problem for a week would put them behind. But in Singapore, they put a premium on thinking about their thinking. They didn't just solve the problem; they probed why the solution worked and how they had gotten to it. This trained their brains to understand how the brain was working. This creation of "habits of the mind," as it has been called by some, is critical to effective learning. That is where the limits of technology come into play. It is very difficult, at this point, for a computer to work with a group of students to help them think about their thinking and to develop practices that are more sound than others. This human aspect of teaching and learning is critical. But I wonder how many of our teachers are taught this way? And how would we need to change our teacher training to strengthen this critical element in teaching?

Although the area of brain research gives us great hope for what may be in education, we have to be careful. It is still a new area of study and the lines from pure research to practice are not always clear. Neuroscientists warn educators not to be too eager to apply what they are learning about the brain directly into the classroom too quickly. A healthy dose of skepticism is also called for. But it is past time we start trying to gingerly apply some of what has been learned to the classroom. As time moves forward, we will know much more about how the brain works and be able to use it to help kids find their dreams.

One of the problems is that educators sometimes confuse brain research with other knowledge that has been generated through developmental psychology and learning theory. The main point here is that brain research is opening new possibilities for our understanding of how the brain functions and learns. Educators need to be attuned to that, but they also need to understand the broader learnings we have about teaching and learning. Knowing for example that previous knowledge and judgments of meaningfulness can influence people's abilities to store new information is important for educators to know. It's also important to understand that breaking learning time into 20-minute segments that are spaced over time is probably better than spending longer blocks trying to master the same material. These understandings come from cognitive psychology not brain research. But the main point here is that the brain is an instrument—a very powerful instrument that can do much more than we previously thought. But that power must be harnessed by other understandings of psychology and learning theory. Altogether, they make for a wonderful tool for educators and should not be ignored.

Pat Wolfe (2003) has had some of the smartest things to say about using brain research. She weds that skepticism with what is known. Some of the things we have learned about how the brain operates can be a helpful guide as long as healthy skepticism is also applied. In Wolfe's article "Brain Research and Education: Fad or Foundation," Wolfe lays out what we do know. It appears that *experience shapes the brain*. Neuroplasticity has shown that the brain we are born with isn't the one we are stuck with. It can be shaped. If nothing else, this should give anyone setting expectations for children with learning problems or from impoverished situations some pause. Some of the strongest connections that are made in the brain come about through concrete learning experiences, which should also give those who push paper and pencil exercises some pause.

We have also learned that *memory is not stored in a single location in the brain*. When an experience enters the brain, it is broken down and distributed to various parts of the cortex. So when you want to recall information, it has to be reconstructed. The implication for this is that the more ways a student has for storing information (seeing, hearing, touching), the more chances they have for creating learning. This seems to support the idea of experiential learning.

Memory is not static. When we learn something, it just doesn't sit in our brains ready for later use. Memory can decay over time, as new information is gained. Comedian Wanda Sykes likened the way we teach school to our brains as an Etch A Sketch. We learn something for a test, and then shake our brains, getting rid of that information to make way for the next thing. This is why we sometimes appear to be ignorant of things we have already learned. However, the Etch A Sketch model is not a given. Wolfe (2003) points out that if we use elaborative rehearsal strategies such as visualizing, writing, symbolizing, singing, semantic mapping, and simulating, we can make more of the learning stick.

Memory is not unitary. There are two different types of memory. One is declarative, which is our everyday memory. It allows us to remember what we had for lunch or where we put our car keys. The other type of memory is procedural memory, which involves habits and skills we have learned such as decoding words, playing tennis, or typing. Procedural learning requires repetition, which is why I am a lousy golfer. I haven't repeated the skills enough. However, repetition isn't a great way to retain declarative learning. Rote learning is great for procedural memory, but elaborative rehearsal is essential for declarative memory. I remember where I put my keys by placing them in certain places regularly so I can find them. Our recollections are at the mercy of our elaborations.

Emotion is a primary catalyst in the learning process. Our amygdale regulates our emotions. It is not an accident that the amygdale is sometimes referred to as the "reptilian brain" or the "ancient brain." It is the base of our humanity and doesn't have knowledge and judgment. It is the source of emotion and our fight-or-flight notions. This means our brains are hardwired to remember those things that have emotions attached to them. However, if we have emotions that are threatening to us, the amygdale readies us to fight or flee—to take action. The emotion becomes dominant over reason at that point, and our rational brain is less efficient. The environment must be safe for us to learn. This is why high-stakes testing is so problematic. It creates an emotional reaction that produces the opposite effect that we are seeking from the student.

Before we leave the topic of the brain, it is also good to take up the issue of the "mind." Much has been said over the years about whether the brain and the mind are the same thing. Philosophers and kings have debated this. Science has explored it. I won't wade into that murky water here, but there is a concept related to the mind that bears understanding. It is what Harvard psychologist Ellen Langer (1989) calls "mindfulness." This is similar to what various eastern religions espouse, but Langer stays away from that issue. She is really talking about *awareness* and *connection*. In her wonderful book called *Mindfulness*, Langer relates a story about a group of elderly people in a nursing home in Connecticut who were given a choice of houseplants to care for and were asked to make a number of small decisions about their daily routines. A year and a half later, not only was this group more cheerful, active, and alert than a similar group who had not been given those choices and responsibilities but, more important, they were still alive. This led her to her research on mindfulness and to its destructive counterpart, mindlessness. Mindless people treat information as though it is context free, regardless of circumstances. This is a state that Langer describes as being one where "the lights are on, but nobody's home." Langer lays out three areas of mindlessness: (1) entrapment by category, (2) automatic behavior, and (3) acting from a single perspective.

If we create new categories, we are operating from a mindful perspective. If we cling to old categories, created in the past, we become mindless. As we become attached to old categories, we harden in our protection of them and become victims to them. This largely describes why wars happen or why issues become intractable—we don't think of new ways of categorizing them.

Automatic behavior occurs when we take in limited signals. Langer describes bumping into a department store mannequin and saying, "Excuse me." It looked like a person, and she hadn't bothered to notice it wasn't a living person. This is often why we do things that are seemingly stupid. At that moment, we *are* stupid because we haven't taken in all the signals. Comedian Bill Engvall who stars in the Blue Collar Comedy Tour and television show and makes numerous personal appearances has a whole routine based on this behavior he calls "Here's your sign." He tells about the time he and his son were flying a kite. A man comes up and says, "Flying a kite?" He answers, "No. We're just fishing for birds. Here's your sign" (Williams & Blomquist, 2003). We just aren't thinking about things actively, and that is the problem.

Acting from a single perspective is acting as though there is only one set of rules. For example, Langer (1989) suggests we moisten our lips with our tongue, and then run our tongue along the back of our teeth, making certain they are nice and moist. It is a pleasant experience. However, if we were asked to spit into a cup and then drink the spit we would find that revolting—even though it is the spit we just used for that very pleasant experience. That is because we have learned that spitting is nasty, and we applied this generalization to our own spit.

The point of all this is that education has to be about more than the brain or even learning theory. It has to be about creating habits of mind to more openness. It is about helping students be more aware of the total picture and taking in various perspectives and not allowing them to harden their categories of understanding. And like those elderly folks in the nursing home, students have to be given responsibilities and choices to remain fully alive. We need to give the students those same kinds of choice if we hope for them ever to engage their brains and minds.

CHAPTER THIRTEEN

Creativity and the Arts

The Surrey, Not the Fringe

Imagination is more important than knowledge.

—Albert Einstein

In this chapter, I will use the arts as a surrogate for the broader issue of creativity. Certainly, creativity can and should be taught in all aspects of the curriculum. Creativity has to be a part of science and technology. It is central to solving all the big human problems. But it is in the arts that creativity has its full flowering, and therefore, the rise and fall of the arts mirrors the concern we have for creativity in general.

Sir Ken Robinson (2001), who headed the British initiative on creativity and was knighted by the queen for his efforts, has been a strong voice for creativity in schools. His case is quite simple. He suggests the economic revolution we are undergoing globally calls for a new conception of human resources, and to develop these resources, we need new strategies. This calls for us to generate new products and services. To create these requires education and training that enables people to be flexible and adaptable so that business can respond to changing markets. Further, people will need to adjust to a world where a secure lifelong job is a rarity. This very utilitarian argument for supporting and promoting creativity is the essence of his book, *Out of Our Minds*. For a very long time, creativity and the arts were promoted because they were fun, and they were a nice add-on to the standard curriculum. Authors and thinkers such as Robinson and Daniel Pink have turned that notion on its head. We must focus on creativity and the arts as if our lives depended on them—because they do.

For years, the arts have been considered an *add-on* to the curriculum of most schools. Lately, with the pressure from standardized tests and shrinking budgets, they have become more of a "subtract-off," with programs being shrunk and cut across the country. This is more than ironic because, at the same time, we are increasingly worried about America's international standing. In fact, it could be argued that the whole reason for the push toward norm-referenced tests grew out of concern for how American children were performing on standardized tests compared to children in other nations. Yet I believe that the reason America has enjoyed its international dominance economically and militarily has as much to do with the "softer" parts of our programs than the harder, more easily measured aspects. Certainly, we have to respect Robinson's (2001) idea that educating more people to higher standards is just part of the solution. We also have to educate them differently, and we can't confuse academic ability with intelligence.

Several years ago, Fareed Zakaria (2008), a columnist for Newsweek, interviewed the minister of education of Singapore about the relative success of the Singaporean students on international tests against the lower success of the American students. Yet as Zakaria pointed out, if you look at these same students years later, it is clear that the Americans are outperforming the Singaporeans in life success—particularly as inventors and entrepreneurs. The minister replied that both countries were meritocracies—Singapore was a meritocracy based on testing, and America was a meritocracy based on talent. He went on to explain that there is not a test for so many of the requisites for success, such as creativity, curiosity, ambition, or sense of adventure. The real key to success comes from a willingness to challenge conventional thinking. Singapore does not emphasize these things and has a way to go to catch America.

Creativity is an outgrowth of culture. If a culture values and supports creativity, it will flourish. If it does not, it will wither away. This conversation between Zakaria and the Singaporean minister took place in the midst of the concerns raised by Thomas Friedman (2005) in his book *The Earth is Flat,* where he outlined the dangers posed by China and India because they have a large number of well-trained engineers and scientists. In fact, as I read his book, I got rather depressed. Because of the size of China and India, they do not need to educate all their children to high levels. A mere 10% would overwhelm the relative smaller number of Americans. Friedman has pointed out that in China you can be one in a million and there will still be a million just like you. In the United States, you can be one in a million and there are only 300 more like you.

But then I remembered the lesson of Singapore and that you don't have to have the most engineers—you just have to have the most innovative and creative ones, and I felt better knowing America's track record for innovation. But then I thought about how we are forfeiting that edge by reducing our emphasis on these areas by cutting out the parts of the curriculum that address them and by emphasizing the parts that speak more to rote recitation and memorization of factoids, and that depressed me again. Creativity flourishes in cultures where people from different back-grounds, perspectives, and expertise are encouraged to interact and share. America's longstanding love affair with diversity has spawned great creative expression. What will happen as the standards movement starts to narrow the funnel of what is important to learn? The problems of the future will not be solved by the solutions from the past. America cannot maintain its greatness by doing more of and better on the things we have historically done. We have to have a renewed commitment to flexibility and lateral thinking. We need less emphasis on making certain everyone achieves the same things and more emphasis on making certain that we are open to different forms of achievement.

A few years ago, I was in a meeting in a town I had never been in before with a group of educators. We had a group dinner in a venue outside of town. One of my friends had a rented car and offered me a ride back to the hotel along with some other friends. Along the way, we ran into some construction and some-how, we got on a freeway going the wrong way. There was a break in traffic, and we didn't notice the danger until we saw a line of headlights headed right at us. After a moment of panic, we swerved off the highway by going off an on-ramp and escaped certain tragedy. As I look down the highway of American education, I often get the same gut-wrenching feeling I got on that distant highway. We are facing disaster because we are going the wrong way. That wrong way is a blind belief that the past is the best road to the future and that more of what hasn't worked well is the solution to what ails us. It is time we got off that road, even if we have to take an on-ramp to get off.

I would argue that we do need real educational transformation, but we do not need to be more like India or China—we need to be more like America. We need to recapture our zeal and openness to creativity and the arts.

As I mentioned earlier, when I first went to Princeton, New Jersey, members of the board came to me individually and strongly "suggested" that I attend the winter concert of the choir. Because my mother had not raised a dummy, I agreed to attend. Princeton had endured some history of conflict over the issue of Christmas and the separation of church and state. They had renamed the Christmas concert the winter concert but had left it in its original venue—the Gothic chapel of Princeton University. At the insistence of the Jewish community, they had also left the song selections alone. These were not the usual seasonal carols but were a mixture of some of the great classical works, many of which had direct religious overtones. The concert, I found out, always ended with Handel's Hallelujah chorus. I was curious to see how such a blatantly religious set of selections had survived the controversy.

I sat in the chapel with its vaulted ceiling rising a hundred feet in the air. A choir came out and started singing. I found that they were quite good and understood why the community had such pride in its music program. After several selections, they left and another group came out, and they were better. In fact, they were probably the best high school choral group I had ever heard. I saw why the board wanted me to witness this event. After several selections, they left, and the lights in the chapel dimmed. A brass quartet took their place in the front and started playing a processional, and from the back, marching in two by two, dressed in robes, and carrying candles, the "real" choir came in singing with such beauty and perfection it made the hair on my neck stand up. I had been seeing the second- and third-string choruses. In that moment, I understood how the program had survived the petty controversies of Christmas celebration. In fact, it has thrived despite them. It was all about excellence. I have already mentioned Bill Trego in an earlier chapter. It is important to note that as superb a teacher as he was, he didn't start the excellence. He merely carried it forward. And when he retired, he was replaced by an equally talented teacher.

The Princeton community had decided many years earlier that excellence in music was a value of the community, and they spread that expectation to the school and the students. All three of my children were gifted with the opportunity to participate in the program. It was easily the most rigorous academic experience they had in school. They had to bring their *A* game every day. They had to learn different languages to sing the music in the original Latin, or German or Italian. They had to collaborate with their friends. They had to learn to follow the precise direction of Mr. Trego. But it wasn't just about him. The district had a second director who was the accompanist for the choir. She was such a talented organist that she went into New York to accompany visiting symphony orchestras who were playing at the Lincoln Center. Trego also directed the male chorus at Princeton University as an "evening" job. The kids were fully aware of the talent their teachers represented and that they were receiving the best instruction available. But it wasn't just the teachers; it was also the commitment of the community that started when the kids were in kindergarten. Every elementary school had a fulltime vocal teacher who was expected to teach sight-reading and the like. The middle school program was so exceptional that when we had the President of Beijing University visiting, he commented that it was the best high school program he had ever seen—and he was listening to our middle school chorus.

The point here is that to get excellence, we have to be committed to creating it. It is about expectations, but it is about so much more. It has to be built from the ground up. And excellence in music isn't just about music, it is about poise, performance under pressure, rising to your highest potential, and creating something no one has ever seen before.

In his wonderful book *A Whole New Mind*, Daniel Pink (2005) argues that we are in the post information age, which he calls the "conceptual age." He argues that, at least, it is a balanced-brain world. After centuries of left-brained dominance, we are now in need of using the right half of the brain as well. He lays out six basic skills for the conceptual world: (1) design, (2) story, (3) symphony, (4) empathy, (5) play, and (6) meaning. He suggests that each of these opens new possibilities for all of us and for future success.

Pink (2005) lays out the idea that with the advent of intelligent technology and cheap, but skillful, labor in emerging Third-World areas, success lies where the work is done and where it cannot be outsourced or given over to technology. For example, for centuries, if people wanted legal documents written or accounting done, the work had to be taken to a specialist. Today, one can buy a program for the home computer to do this. But if you want something designed to be more beautiful or more efficient, that must be done by people who have access to their right brain. The implications for education in this are staggering. That is why I suggest that the arts are not the fringe on the surrey. They are not a mere adornment for looking good—they are the essence of education, the vehicle for getting us where we need to go.

As I thought about the power of our creativity and the difference it might make in the successful future of America, I thought about the kinds of creative expression we had given the world. Take music for example: We have offered jazz, blues, bluegrass and country, gospel, rhythm and blues, rock and roll, hip-hop, and rap to name a few. What do all these musical forms have in common? They came from those who were "left behind" in our culture. They came from the edges of our society. But take this idea further. What about the Native American population? Ask a young Native American to solve a difficult math equation, and she may struggle. Ask her to design something for you, and you find they are amazing designers—something Dan Pink (2005) suggests is one of the six basic skills in the conceptual age. If you go into a classroom full of immigrant children, you will often find them struggling academically, yet they code shift, culture shift, and language shift many times during the day—something most middle-class Americans cannot do, despite the need for a global perspective. Ask a young man slouched on a street corner in any major city what he thinks of systems thinking. You will likely draw a blank expression. Put him on a basketball court, and he knows where 10 people are while moving through time and space and can anticipate their moves and create elegant solutions to them—systems thinking. And yet we tend to devalue what these children are bringing to the school setting, and so we spend a lot of time telling them what they don't know and what they can't do instead of building on the creativity they bring and helping them bridge that to the broader skills necessary to succeed.

Author Richard Florida (2002) has written about the emergence of a "creative class" in America. He estimates that nearly 40 million Americans are part of that class. This is a tenfold increase from 100 years ago, and it has doubled since 1980. This push toward increased emphasis and reliance on creativity is taking place around the world. Japan, known mostly for its emphasis on a strict adherence to rules and tradition, is emphasizing creativity in its schools. The United Kingdom estimates that the creative sector is producing 200 billion dollars worth of goods and services each year. The explosion of creativity grows out of the increased power of technology to do the work previously handled by the left, sequential, logical side of the brain and from the availability of educated and cheap labor overseas. But most important, the evolution of society toward one that is more focused on meaning and play calls for more entertainment. Entertainment must be created. And the complexity and inherent danger in today's world calls for more creativity.

In his stunning and disturbing book *The Age of the Unthinkable*, author Joshua Cooper Ramo (2009) explores the vast changes in society over the last several centuries. He concludes that the old rules no longer apply in economics, politics, diplomacy, or warfare. This calls for a very different approach. Ramo points out that we are keeping our problems out of sight and hidden. We should be confronting them. He quotes Robert Unger who said, "The task of imagination is to do the work of crisis without crisis" (Unger quoted in Ramo, p. 254). So we have a choice between imagination and crisis. This alone is why we need to focus more on the creative side of things. Self-help guru Wayne Dyer (2004) points out that "when you change the way you look at things, the things you look at change" (p. 173). If we are looking at a world of uncertainty and possible crisis, then we need to make certain that we are changing how we look at things. Ramo suggests that wealth in the new world must be measured not by money or power but by the ability to change and adapt—the essence of creativity. He suggests you should measure what you have with what you can do. He also states that resilience has to be the goal of our society and that relationships are critical to success. This is true at the macrolevel, but it is also true person to person. In school, we have been so focused on outcomes that we have forgotten to consider the human producing the outcome. A focus on creativity and the softer parts of learning can reconnect us to that human element.

Ramo (2009) goes further to state that the moment you hand over power to other people you get an explosion of creativity, innovation, and effort. This has tremendous implications for how schools are governed and how much control the federal and state government should have over what happens in school. It even has implications for classroom teachers who want to keep a tight rein on what the kids are doing. If we want more creativity (and we must have it to survive), we need to back our efforts by freeing people to do what they can do—to create the changes that need to be created. Further, the more users a decentralized system has the more efficient it becomes because the work can be spread out and done by whomever can do it best and fastest.

Further, our very future is at risk as we ignore the solutions made possible by creative expression. Our society has become one where punishment and blame have become more important than affirmation and support. We spend more and more money each year on fixing problems than on preventing them. The old joke educators used to tell is that it costs more to put someone in the state pen than to send them to Penn State is so past the point of relevance that it is hardly repeated these days. State budgets are being overwhelmed by prison costs while education remains stagnant. We spend much more on treating the sick than doing prevention with the healthy so they don't become sick. This tendency is repeated in the area of creativity and the arts. We view them as add-ons and frills when they are the source of many of the solutions we lack and need.

The popular view of intelligence is memorization and the accumulation of facts. Television shows such as *Jeopardy*, *Who Wants to Be a Millionaire?* and *Are you Smarter than a Fifth Grader?* speak to the popular culture's fixation with people who can remember many things. The Academy Award-winning movie *Slumdog Millionaire* showed just how empty this notion is. The young man at the center of the movie wins on the Indian version of *Who Wants to Be a Millionaire?* not because he has a prodigious memory but because fate had given him certain lessons that just happened to be the answers to the questions he faced on the show. The moral is that fate is more powerful than memorization. Yet we continue to pursue educational policies that try to make all our children contestants on these shows while all our fates lie in their hands.

A real premium should be put on teaching them how to learn and, just as important, how to look at problems in new ways. The old-fashioned surrey with the fancy fringe is as irrelevant as the old style of education that emphasizes rote learning and a focus on factoids. But it would be good to remember what is central and what is just for show. The fringe was pretty but meaningless. The surrey is what got you someplace. In the world of tomorrow, it will be those nations and those individuals who have the ability to create who will drive the future.

CHAPTER FOURTEEN

Authentic Accountability

Not everything that can be counted, counts, and not everything that counts can be counted.

—Albert Einstein

For the past couple of decades, there has been an increasing interest in making schools more accountable. There has been a sense that if accountability is increased, then schools will improve. The problem with this thinking is that it assumes that the problems schools face are internal and that results can be changed simply through external pressure that will change internal behavior. In essence, it implies that the educational problems facing America are rooted solely in the schools and that by increasing the heat on schools it will force better performance. It is not unlike finding that your car is not running well and then you step on the gas to get it to run faster without looking into why it may be sputtering. Perhaps there is a serious problem with the engine or dirt in the gas line or there is no gas at all. The problems with cars are complex. The problems with schools are beyond complexity.

It is difficult to argue against a sense of accountability. First, schools are funded by the public and serve the public's interest, so they need to be accountable to the public. The problem with the current accountability system is that it makes schools accountable to state and federal bureaucrats at the behest of state and federal political figures. From a purely practical point, most of the funding for schools comes from local sources in most states, and therefore, it would make sense that schools should be accountable to those who pay the bills and are most interested in the outcome—the abilities of children.

This is further complicated by the fact that the business community has become very involved in the discussion because they argue that the failure of the schools leads to economic decline. They want workers who have world-class skills, and they feel the schools are not producing them. There is a problem with all this. Schools are there for more than economic ends, and the ends the business community desire from the schools will not be generated by simply having more students score higher on tests. When business is asked about the kind of workers they need, they mention basic skills, but they express a greater need for workers who are innovative, collaborative, and responsible. None of those things show up on the current accountability scorecards.

The problem with the expectation of the political community is that they think current school results are caused by a poor attitude on the part of school people. If we could simply get their attitudes right, then the results would improve. Of course, the problem with this thinking is that, for the most part, most educators already would like to see their kids do better. They hardly need a spanking to want that to happen. The second issue is that the assumption that test scores have some direct correlation to success in life is not there. Simply relying on an outcome-based approach will not get us the results we need.

The advent of the No Child Left Behind version of the Elementary and Secondary Education Act ratcheted up this discussion. It required all schools and all students to operate at a proficient level by 2014. Although the intent was certainly admirable, there are serious questions as to its practicality. And as mentioned in earlier chapters, the result of an intense focus on outcomes in reading and math caused a distortion in the teaching and curriculum. As any farmer knows, you can't fatten a pig by weighing it, and every teacher knows you can't make children smarter simply by testing them. It takes food to fatten and support to smarten. This emphasis on testing meant other things that were not tested started being less attended to—the very things that the business community suggests it needs to be competitive internationally. Proponents of the law point out, rightfully so, that the imperative in the law to disaggregate data based on race, social class, and learning ability caused school systems to attend more carefully to the needs of students who may have formerly been "left behind." There is truth to that claim, but the question remains whether improved emphasis on low-order test results really helps those students in the long run. This assumes that there is a strong correlation between test results and overall student achievement. Researchers, such as Sharon Nichols and David Berliner (2007), have shown that while scores improved on state tests, they did not improve on international or college admission tests. The old saying from supporters of testing is that "whatever gets tested gets taught." This is true, but the obverse is also true—in a coercive accountability system, whatever doesn't get tested does not get taught. In a world where skills such as creativity and innovation are key, what happens to those students who leave school with better state test results but who cannot function in this higher-order environment? Further, although low-income students are getting more attention, there has been a rising concern about the gifted and other students who are getting less attention and what that might mean for our competitiveness in the long run.

The bottom line is that although there needs to be accountability, we need to make certain that we are using an *authentic* approach to it—one that generates the outcomes we need and our children deserve. Much has been said by the supporters of a stronger accountability system on how American students perform against children from other countries. The irony is that I have found in my international travel that the countries that have had a major emphasis on test results are starting to drift away from that model to one that puts a higher premium on innovative thinking. We seem to be moving in the opposite direction.

This was brought home to me on a visit to the Irish Republic a couple of years ago. At that time, the economic "Celtic tiger" was roaring with a booming economy at home and great strides being made internationally. Recent economic downturns have abated that somewhat, but there is no doubt that Ireland is on the rise. In a meeting with the minister of education for Ireland, she emphasized the role education played in that success. We had learned that their accountability system was strong and very different from our own. It was called Quality Assurance, and it involved a collaborative approach between the federal government and the local schools. The government saw it as a partnership, and its job was not merely to point out weaknesses but to work with the local schools to increase their capacity to address those weaknesses. The focus was not just on student achievement in the narrow sense we were used to it in the United States, but the accountability system looked at a broad range of issues including even parent and community involvement.

I asked the minister about how they handled testing. Her reply was instructive. She said,

> But of course, we test. It is important for the teachers to know how the kids are doing. But we would never release the scores publicly. Because you know, if we did that, what would happen. The newspapers would publish the results and compare the schools, and we know which ones will do worse—the ones with lots of poor children. Why would we want to subject our teachers, who are working so hard with those children, to criticism and ridicule? (personal communication)

I suggested to the Minister that perhaps she might want to come to America and share that philosophy.

The point is that I am sure the Irish system could be better just as we could. But its assumptions are very different than the assumptions that underpin our system of accountability. They assume that it should be collaborative, promote growth in a positive way, and not act punitively. This is almost the exact opposite of how we handle accountability. The Irish system looks at things like professional development and learning supports. They worry about the quality of management, the quality of planning, and the quality of teaching and learning. Now current proponents of the external, top-down system of accountability in the United States would call these things "inputs" and suggest that they are not appropriate for an accountability system. I would suggest they are not inputs but "throughputs"—the very things that make a difference in the classroom. Their focus is not on what is put into the classroom or what comes out of it—they focus on what happens inside the classroom.

It is true that we had to move away from simply measuring how much we gave schools. The problem is we went to measuring what we could measure, which was simple outputs. The real test of effectiveness happens inside the classroom, and we need an accountability system that considers that. We know that there are teaching practices that are more effective than others. We know there are management practices that are more effective than others. We know that an environment where a child feels connected and that connection comes with cooperation between the home and school is the most effective system we could produce. All these things should be part of an authentic accountability system.

We have to take a broader view of accountability than we currently have. When the public is asked about accountability, they want to know more than the test results. They want to know how the money is being spent. They want to know how welcome they are at the school and how involved they might become. We have conflated student achievement with accountability, and we have confused test results with student achievement. Accountability is more than student achievement, and student achievement is more than test results. I believe that parents are looking at test results simply because they have so few other things to look at.

When I was in Tucson, we had a magnet school that was so popular parents signed up their kids as soon as they knew they were expecting a baby. It was the school everyone wanted their child to go to. But as a superintendent who was worried about test results, I couldn't quite understand why. You see, the test results of the school put them in the middle of the pack. The school did not have outstanding outcomes in our system of accountability. I decided to spend some time to see what was happening. I found a school running over with enthusiasm. Kids were excited and happy. The school was full of parents volunteering to help. It was full of student artwork, and kids were moving all about the school doing their work with smiles on their faces. It was like the school I would later visit in New Zealand. Although the Disney folk like to claim that Disneyland is the happiest place on earth, I have seen schools and classrooms that could give them a run for their money. This school was one of them.

I told the principal I was very impressed but couldn't understand why his test scores weren't higher. He chuckled and said, "Our scores will be higher when you test what we teach." He then pulled out a file of a first grader. He showed me her writing sample from September. It was a couple of lines. He then showed me work from December. It was a couple of paragraphs. He showed me work from March, and it was a couple of pages. He then explained that one of the values of the school was writing fluency—something that was not on any of the tests we gave in the district. He then asked me would I have him not teach that. Of course, he had me on the spot, and he had given me a very powerful lesson on why our current accountability model is a problem.

First, we don't necessarily test what we teach. In many states, there is a low correlation between curriculum and tests given. And more important, we don't always test what is most important—often because there isn't yet a test to do that. The parents were happy with that school in Tucson, first, because they were there in the school and could see what was being taught. And more important, they could see the smiles on their children's faces everyday when they came home. The test results were but a poor proxy for what they could see with their own eyes. I think most parents want test results because they want to know something good has happened to their children because they realize that far too often schools are places of monotony and boredom. Authentic accountability has to grow out of an authentic approach to school. It has to be meaningful, first and foremost, to the students who go there. And it has to be meaningful to the parents who entrust their children to that school. All the rest is merely sound and fury, signifying not so much.

CHAPTER FIFTEEN

Lead Is Not a Four-Letter Word

A leader is a dealer in hope.

—Napoleon Bonaparte

To make the transformation required to create schools worthy of our children will require a new kind of leadership. Historically, school leaders rose up through the ranks of teaching and then various levels of administration. This allowed them to be steeped in the work of schools and what has been, but it also was a tie to the past that could blind them to the possibilities of what might be. Of late, we have seen a different kind of leader emerge. These are people who have not spent time in schools aside from attending them, but they have been leaders in other realms—business, military, and the like. This nontraditional model of leader brings in a new perspective and allows these people to look at the problems with fresh eyes and a different lens. However, because they have no depth in the work of schools, they approach schools as an amateur might approach flying an airplane.

Over the years, I have flown hundreds of thousands of miles myself. You might call me an expert flyer. Every time I board a plane, there is a set routine. I walk down the jet way to be greeted by a flight attendant who welcomes me aboard. I look to the left and the door to the cockpit is open. I can see the pilots going through their preflight rituals. I turn right, walk down the aisle, and find my seat. I am proud to say that I have never once been tempted to turn left, walk into the cockpit, and announce that because of my extensive experience as a passenger I am going to fly the plane today. It would be very foolish to put me in the pilot seat and let me try to fly you to Cleveland. I doubt we would make it, despite my thousands of hours of flying experience. Yet we are putting people into leadership roles in schools whose main claim to expertise in education is that they once attended school. Amateurs, although bringing an open perspective to the problems, lack an understanding of the complexity of the institutions they are leading. Not a good thing. The romance we have had the last few years with amateur leaders in education hasn't really yielded the breakthroughs people had hoped for. So if experienced educators are too locked in on the status quo to be effective, and if nontraditional leaders are too simplistic to be effective, what is the answer? I think it comes from looking at the kinds of thinking needed to lead schools in today's environment. Both traditional and nontraditional leaders might be effective if they were looking at the issue with clearer eyes.

Developing great leaders for tomorrow's schools should be approached much as I am suggesting we approach students. They need to be engaged in meaningful activities. They need to be given *ways of thinking* that allow them to look for solutions outside the box of their experience. First, we have to see that the role itself is different. Traditional leaders spend much of their training learning how to deal with the problems that exist today. In that regard, their training is making them more effective mechanics. They are learning how to tinker with what is. But what if "what is" is irrelevant to the current needs? It is like spending a lot of time fixing the car when you really should be flying a plane. I would suggest that if leaders want to give wings to children's dreams they must not think like carpenters—they need to think more like architects. They have to understand design, and they need to be inventive in creating new ways of seeing and doing.

You have to start with the design of things and then move forward. As I have said before, if you start with the understanding that the schools we presently have are perfectly designed to yield the results we are getting and you are unhappy with the results, it is a design problem. But because the world is changing so rapidly, it becomes an ongoing design issue. Schools have been caught up in the idea of continuous improvement, but the real issue is the need for continuous conception.

I have also thought that we needed to stop seeing school leaders as chief operating officers and start seeing them as something else entirely. One of the fallacies of the nontraditional school leader movement is that it doubles-down on the CEO expectation for leaders. The criticism has been that schools and school systems are big organizations that require someone who is good at managing organizations. So a manager of a set of stores or a leader honed in the military would make a better CEO than someone who just came out of the classroom because a teacher lacks the requisite managerial skills to lead the organization. That might be true if that were really the job. The problem is that schools are not factories or battalions. They have a very complex output—children. Further, the role of school is also social. So part of the output is creating citizens for a complex and diverse democracy. It is also to provide workers prepared for a quickly changing work environment. It must be considered that while children are the output of the organization, that makes the inputs quite varied. There is no quality control on raw materials. And the very quality of the material is shaped by a number of forces outside the purview of the school.

Also, the schools exist in a political environment, so although school leaders may be responsible, they are not in charge. I spoke with a former general who was running a large urban school district, and he told me that he had fought in three wars and had never faced anything like trying to lead a school district. The district needed to close a number of schools because of excess space and inefficiencies. That was an easy call for him. He ordered them closed. Then the community was in an uproar. He had not followed a process of community involvement. Elected officials got involved, and he had to back down. Another high profile urban superintendent who had been a businessman, a governor, and a national political leader said that being superintendent was the hardest job he had ever had. And although the principalship is not as complex, its issues are more deeply embedded and harder to confront. So I am not convinced we need a CEO model of school leadership.

As the son of a Methodist minister, I grew up looking through his lens, and as a former principal and superintendent, I think it is a useful perspective. Part of the role of school leader is more ministerial than anything else. Certainly, real school leadership must be purpose driven. I suggest that it is really more of a mission or calling than anything else. When you are responsible for the lives of children and for shepherding their dreams, you have a powerful mission. Although you have little formal authority in the job, because in education accountability is centralized but authority is dispersed, you have powerful moral authority because of the role you play. Further, the minister's effectiveness comes from the power to convene and persuade. That is also what a school leader can do. The first task of school leaders is to recognize the limits of their formal power and to exploit the expanses of their informal power. So looking, first and foremost, at the job as an opportunity to *serve* has to be the starting place.

If the task of leadership is not in a "command and control" mode, then what is it? I think it is really about collaborating and communicating. The real power of school leaders is to find ways of using their informal power to bring people together. The skill set has to be around creating collaborative processes. It is also about effectively communicating the challenges and possibilities. By doing so, school leaders can help their community create the vision for what they want their schools to be. That means leaders have to be able to work both inside and outside the school to bring all the players together.

It is about connecting the dots for those in the system and those that the system serves. I have always marveled at looking at a starry night sky. One of the reasons is the realization that, thousands of years ago, someone looked at the same sky and noticed that if you drew imaginary lines between the stars you would see rams and crabs and people. School leaders have to be in that same sort of sense-making business. They have to connect the dots for others. School leaders exist in a chaotic environment. Therefore, leaders must be flexible. They have to make sense of things for themselves and for those who work with them. Because they stand on higher ground, leaders are capable of seeing further and with better understanding of the interplay of forces that affect their work than those who are looking from a more limited perspective. But to do so, they must be able to step back from their work and reflect on what is happening. Currently, there are few training programs for school leaders that emphasize *reflective practice*, and yet that is at the core of the new kind of leadership that is needed in today's context, and certainly, it is critical for leading the organization to a new place.

A few years ago, I was diagnosed with glaucoma. I didn't know much about it except that it was a disease of the eyes, and it wasn't a good thing to have. As I learned more about it, I found that it stemmed from excess fluid pressure inside the eye, which as it built up, started damaging the optic nerve. It is a very insidious disease because it works gradually and painlessly. You really aren't aware of it, and as it continues its damage, the vision is affected, first at the periphery. You lose your sense of things at the edge of your world. If not arrested, the patient develops tunnel vision and can eventually go blind. As I learned more about glaucoma, I realized what a perfect metaphor it is for the challenges leaders face. Leaders are under constant pressure. They make thousands of little decisions every day. If you don't pull back and consider their interplay and effect, you can start to lose your vision as a leader, and eventually, you will be blinded and incapable of helping the organization. That is why reflective practice becomes so important. Just stepping back from the day-to-day decisions to think about their impact allows the leader to get in front of events. It is ironic that sometimes the best way of moving forward is to step back, but that is exactly what reflective practice is about. There are many ways to become a reflective practitioner: You can write or keep a journal of your work; you can choose to mentor a prospective leader, who will ask you the critical question of *why* did you do something; or you can teach a course to others. The important thing is to create a system that forces you to step back and think about what you are doing.

In fact, one of the basic skills of the new leader comes from understanding that their lives are bathed in irony. They are surrounded by paradox. Richard Farson (1997), author of the book *Management of the Absurd: The Paradoxes of Leadership*, once suggested to me that if school leaders, most particularly superintendents, were solving problems, there was something wrong in their organizations. Every problem that has a solution should be solved lower in the organization. The person on top is dealing with paradoxes that have no solution. Their job is to wrestle with dilemmas that have no clear outcome. When he told me that, suddenly, all those years I spent as a superintendent made sense to me for the first time. That is exactly how I spent my time—dealing with issues that didn't seem to have a clear or totally positive outcome. It reminded me of a comment that Jonathan Kozol (personal communication) once made about the urban school superintendent. He suggested that urban superintendents were simply "mediating injustice." How does one keep his or her sanity and soul under this condition? I think it must come from understanding the complexity of the role and that it requires the ability to step back, weigh all the angles, and then move forward toward what is sometimes the best of a bad set of alternatives.

I don't want to suggest that the role of leader in today's context is all full of darkness and despair. I am just suggesting that the life of a leader who thinks they have all the answers will not be a happy one. In his book *The Age of the Unthinkable,* author Joshua Cooper Ramo (2009) suggests that the ability to change and adapt are critical in the quickly shifting sands of events. He uses the metaphor of the Christmas box. He points out that often children will ignore the expensive present to play with the box it came in. The reason is that is the present, such as a Barbie doll, has limited use, but the box has unlimited potential. Modern leadership must not only know how to get out of the box but how to make multiple uses of it—how to play with it. Author Roberto Unger (Unger in Ramo, 2009) suggests that the task of imagination is to do the work of crisis without crises. Ramo suggests that is the choice that we have now: imagination or crisis.

So how can a leader begin to move from the current crises we face in schools? Quite simply, it is to move away from accepting the current model as a given and begin seeking new models. New leaders need to have keen imaginations and the willingness and courage to use it. They must have the skills to help others see the possibilities and to energize them to work toward them. All this will require a different kind of training for leaders. I believe that school leaders must be steeped in a variety of disciplines—economics, demographics, anthropology, political science, and the like. Further, they must be taught to think differently.

After I completed my master's degree, I began working on my doctorate. One of the classes I took was school law. I learned about the various cases and the necessity to avoid tort as much as possible. I then applied to study at Harvard, and when I got there, I found that I had to start over with my classes—Harvard didn't accept transfer credits, and once again, I had to take school law. Except this time, the training was all about *thinking* like a lawyer. I learned, to my surprise, that the law wasn't a fixed idea—it was what very human judges said it was. I learned that the Supreme Court did not operate outside the political lines, but very much inside them. And most important, I learned to look at issues as a lawyer might look at them. Later, when I became a superintendent, I saved the districts I worked for lots of money because I knew how to talk with our attorneys and how to frame the discussion for maximum result. This is just an example of how leaders need to learn, not just the content of the disciplines they study but the thinking that drives the content. School leaders have to be facile connoisseurs of different ways of thinking. In doing so, they can begin to lead their organizations into providing children with that same skill set. It isn't so much about what we know but how we came to know it and what we can do with it once it is evident to us. That is the new way of learning and leading.

Over the last few years, I have done a lot of thinking and writing about the concept of spiritual leadership. In fact, I coauthored a book, *The Spiritual Dimension of Leadership*, with Steven Sokolow (Houston & Sokolow, 2006) that looks at some of the spiritual principles that undergird leadership. Spiritual leadership is a way of looking beneath the surface of issues to the underlying operational system, so to speak. Einstein once suggested that no problem is ever solved at the level it was created. You have to look at the underlying level. For example, schools today are faced with massive financial issues. It is good to keep in mind that financial crisis in public institutions are really issues of values—how much does a community or state value its children? In the richest country in the world, despite recent economic setbacks, the real question of adequate funding for schools revolves around how much people value the children around them. Sometimes leaders are called to make this clearer to people.

At the very practical level, spiritual principals underlie the work of the leader. Although *delegation* is considered a basic skill of leadership, if the leader cannot trust the people she has delegated to and be willing to forgive them for not doing the work the way the leader might have done it, the leader will always be a micromanager. Further, because leadership in today's turbulent times is really an act of whitewater rafting, leaders need to understand that there is an underlying system that allows them to know where they should be headed. Several years ago, Deepak Chopra (2002) pointed out in the American Association of School Administrator's (AASA) *School Administrator* that "leaders are the symbolic soul of the groups they lead. Leaders can thrive on chaos if they understand the underlying spiritual order. Choosing to lead is choosing to step out of the darkness."

Throughout this book, I have suggested that we don't need to reform our schools—we need to transform them. We need to take what is there and make something entirely different out of that. For that to happen, the single biggest influence will be the leaders who are working in the schools. Transformation and change are inside jobs. They must come from the very organizations that must change, and the only way that will happen is if school leaders step up and *lead.*

CHAPTER SIXTEEN

Bored of Education

*God made the idiot for practice
and then he made the school board.*

—Mark Twain

There is no topic of conversation that is likely to elicit more discussion at a meeting of educators than raising the issue of school boards. Even policymakers have weighed in on the issue of school governance. Before wading into this swamp of opinion, perhaps a little history is in order.

When common schools were created in the United States, they were created largely by states that immediately passed on their responsibilities to local communities who created school boards or school committees to oversee the operation of schools. As things became more complex, these committees selected a fulltime person to take on this role and that was the birth of school superintendents. It was also the beginning of tensions over who should run the schools. The real point here is that school boards were a creature of their community and were there to express the community's hopes and dreams for their children. The other main point is that this was the genesis of local control of schools—a recognition that those closest to the children know best what they need.

In the early days, these school governance structures were made of community leaders. In the rural areas, they were often the most successful farmers. In the cities, they were the business leaders in the community. Typically, they worked closely with the superintendent or principals in the smaller communities. They gave over the day-to-day oversight to the professional leaders and met briefly to set budgets and make broad policy. In the middle of the last century, with the emergence of teacher unions, civil rights, and growing discord over the quality and direction of schools, a more grassroots board emerged made of community activists, parents, and those elected with the support of teacher unions. The governance process became more combative, and the community elites that once ran the systems began to withdraw. Many business titans no longer lived in the communities where their businesses existed. Others felt too busy to take on the civic responsibility, and still others were put-off with the heated conflicts that grew around the schools. Of course, there are still vestiges of this model of elite governance left, but it tends to be in the wealthier suburbs and the more stable rural communities. It is rare to find an urban district governed by elites.

Further, during the mid-1960s, a spate of actions from the federal government around education and major court cases impinged on the flexibility of school boards. As calls for more accountability rose, states started taking back their prerogatives from the local communities, and the legislature and state boards started taking on the governance for schools in determining what was taught and how it was taught. Toward the latter part of the 20th century, the federal government stepped up its intrusion into schooling. Its role had started with the passage of the Elementary and Secondary Education Act (ESEA) in the early 1960s and was increased in the 1970s with the passage of the Individuals with Disabilities Education Act (IDEA), overseeing the rights and responsibilities toward handicapped children. Much more followed—laws to protect the rights of the disabled, court cases around bilingual education, and the like. In the first year of the 21st century, the reauthorization of ESEA took the name No Child Left Behind and took significant control of what happened in schools. All this further curtailed the ability of local boards to oversee the schools in their communities.

Meanwhile, the strife between board members was increasingly covered in the local media. Single-issue candidates, candidates representing special-interest groups, or people who ran for their needs created conflict among board members and caused some who were there for civic purposes to leave in disgust. Others felt hemmed in by the impact of state and federal intervention and by the power of teacher unions. Phil Schlechty (person communication), a prolific writer and thinker on education, best summarized this to me as he discussed the history of boards. He said that in the past, board members ran to serve the public, and now they seem to run to be served by the public. All of this is an overly generalized description of the current state of things. In my conversations with superintendents, many brag about the positive qualities of their boards and the great functionality of their work. But often, as I probe these comments, I find they are speaking relatively comparing them to other boards in their area that are highly dysfunctional.

There are many problems with the current model. One of the greatest is the lack of clarity regarding expectations. It is not always clear to boards what they should do, and they pass that down by being unclear about their expectations. This has been described as being asked by a board to bring them the proverbial dog. When the dog appears, they make it clear that they want a small dog, not a big one. When the small dog is produced, they complain that they want a small white one, not a small black one, and on and on. If expectations are made with more clarity upfront, great time, effort and frustration would be spared. The lack of specificity is a huge issue. This often comes from boards focusing on the wrong things. If they focus on the small picture and worry about managing the details of the system, then they will not have a clear picture of the larger focus needed. This lack of clarity can ultimately lead to confusion and conflict.

There are any numbers of board member or superintendent behaviors that can also lead to problems. A level of mistrust between boards and management will not do either group much good. There has to be a commitment to a strong working relationship between the two. This means that communications have to be clear and that there should be some rules as to who is authorized to speak and what they can say. If you have individual members of the board going off about personal agendas, it creates problems for the administration and the other members of the board. There should be clear expectations that board members have ways of dealing with one another to avoid bickering, and they should have realistic expectations for the superintendent. Just because the title has "super" in it doesn't make them superheroes! When superintendents are hired, they are often expected to be all things to all people. This is unrealistic and can lead to disillusionment and conflict.

Boards need to keep focused on the bigger picture and should be the question people not the answer people. They are there to give guidance and clarity. They can best do that by reasonable and respectful questioning of management to make certain that the district is heading in the right direction. They should be selecting the destination, not acting as a backseat driver. The role of governance is to identify problems and issues, not to give the solutions. As much as possible, they should be the people who determine *what* is taught but not be directing *how* it is taught. They must also act as a buffer for the staff to keep the community from overrunning the system. When a board can act in this more high-minded way, things will go smoothly. When they can't, it can be a very rocky ride and can create real confusion and controversy.

All this controversy has led to frustration with the system and the creation of "work-arounds" to get past the problems. The growth of charter schools is as much about getting around or away from the system of governance as anything else. In many ways, it is a reaffirmation of the early history of schools when they were very local and very reflective of the desires of those sending their children to them. I have always found it ironic that the very politicians who advocate for charter schools and breaking the bonds of governance are the ones who created many of these bonds to begin with. Much of the bureaucratic behavior and rules attached to schools come from outside the local governance structure. We have also seen a spate of mayoral control activities, where mayors are given much greater control of the schools in their communities. In some cases, where the mayors are strong and very interested in schools and can work in harmony with their superintendents, this seems to have worked. In others, it has simply moved the problem to a different location.

So what is the proper role of governance, if any? Clearly, schools are more than the sum of their parts. They are not simply places where children go to learn to read or write. They are the expression of the hopes and dreams of parents and the larger community for what the future can become through the work of the children. If that is true, then there is clearly a role for the community to express itself about its schools. Part of the real problem with much of today's reform agenda is that it has moved the locus of control away from those closest to the children. Of course, there have always been abuses of local control. History shows that many local boards in the south were very recalcitrant when it came to integrating the schools. There is ample history that inequalities still abound in districts and in states. There are multiple examples of nepotism and corruption, so local control is not always idyllic.

However, people left to solve their own problems tend to be creative in their approach. I believe it can be argued that local control has been one of those engines that have driven education quality in the United States. No governor or legislator is smarter about what children need than the parents, teachers, and administrators who work with them can be. More than anything else, what has been missing is a common set of expectations and a system that will allow one community to learn from another. I don't believe this will come from coercive legislation or top-down decision making. Perhaps the emergence of a national set of standards will help if the local schools are left to figure out how to meet them and are given the capacity to do so. Time will tell. Ironically, in this era of accountability, the local governance system could be the core of reasonable accountability—if they were allowed to do their work and if they can stay focused on the right things.

Any good school needs four things from its district leadership: (1) clarity, (2) capacity, (3) coherence, and (4) constancy. This is needed from district leadership and, most of all, from the governance structure. Clarity is the "vision thing," as President George H. W. Bush called it. It is providing the sense of knowing what can be done and what can be gained by connecting to the community and then stating that knowledge in ways that everyone understands. Then the system can be galvanized into action toward this vision. The single school is too small of a unit to provide this, and the state is too far away. Vision that is too close to the action lacks broader context, and vision that is from too great a distance is distorted and faint. The role of leadership, when it comes to vision, is to listen to the community and interpret what it is saying into words that the community understands and can rally around.

Capacity provides the resources and muscle to get the work done. Site-level reform often flounders because there are just not enough resources at one school to do the job. The lack of scale forces the school to do without needed resources to create the infrastructure to make the work effective. Change can only come to schools when the governance and leadership moves from a command-and-control model to one that builds capacity.

Coherence and constancy help the schools make sense out of what is happening and shows the understanding that real reform takes time. The problem with any kind of bottom-up reform, including charter schools, is that it fails to recognize that, in our complex society, people don't stay in one place year to year. In many urban districts, students move when the rent comes due and the parents can't pay it. They move to another location and start fresh. If there is no coherence in the system, then the new start can be fraught with problems. State- and federal-level guidance is far too removed to be of any help on the ground. No school is an island, and real reform must come on a broader scale. A solid governance model can go far in making this a reality. Likewise, real change is bigger than one principal or one faculty. Certainly, heroic leadership can get things started, but what happens when the hero leaves? If there is not a system in place to keep it going, the dramatic changes falter and fail. Change requires the will to stay the course. They must emanate from the governance structure.

In the last few years, there have been attempts to modify the governance structure of schools. States, such as Massachusetts and Kentucky, have passed sweeping legislation to dictate what boards can and cannot do. Much of this has had to do with the personnel powers of boards. It has been my experience that this is often the point of greatest friction between management and governance. Usually, there are pretty extensive processes for hiring, transferring, and firing personnel. When lay boards insert themselves into this process, it can often lead to major complications. At the worst end of the spectrum is nepotism and corruption, with boards getting their family or friends hired or being paid for their votes. Far more often, however, it is just the overriding of the processes, the lack of knowledge of the candidates, and the confusion that arises as to whom folks work for once they are hired that caused, at least, these two states to curtail the personnel powers of boards and limited them to hiring and overseeing the contract of the superintendent who then is responsible for the system personnel.

There have also been some attempts to limit what items a board can and cannot oversee. There have been suggestions to limit the number of meetings a year the board can have. I once had a board that met over 180 times in one year. Meeting that often is not about policy—it is about managing, and that is where the confusion and conflict arise. However, I think merely setting limits on meetings won't get the job done. We need a new metaphor.

Some have suggested the metaphor of corporate boards, but with recent economic meltdowns that model has lost some of its luster. Others have suggested the hospital or utilities model. Hospital boards are clearly circumscribed from making medical decisions. They set general policy and direction and oversee finances. The utility model has some attraction. They meet a limited number of times a year to set overall direction. In many cases, they are representative of the public, which is very important to the democratic practice. As mentioned early, in some cases, it has just been turned over directly to the politicians, but this model is clearly an invitation to politicizing the process even further. It works when a mayor has insight and sensitivity to the issues. It doesn't when she does not.

What is clear is that there is no real clarity on how schools can and should be governed. It is also clear, to me, that we should have a model that reflects the community's desires and dreams working in collaboration with the professionals in the system. Education is too important to be left to the educators. But it is also too complex to be left to the amateurs. A model that takes the best from both is one that we should be striving toward. I lean toward a model that has community input in the selection of the board, with the board having powers limited to the most important things about education—who leads the system, what should be taught, what the overall expectations the community has for its children, and oversight of the resources. Although governance is not and should not be "exciting," it is too important not to be considered as a major part of any reform effort.

It could be argued that if we are to transform our schools into places that are worthy of our children, change has to begin at the governance level. Without a functioning board that can take the desires of the community and work with the educators to create a system that will translate those desires into reality, and without a board that will run interference with those who would try to undermine and block the changes necessary for transformation, real change is impossible. I have a friend who reminded me that change is an inside job, and changing the inside of a system has to start with those who lead it.

CHAPTER SEVENTEEN

Dealing With the Heart and Soul

If you work with your hands, you are a laborer. If you work with your hands and your head, you are a craftsman. If you work with your hands, your head, your heart and soul, you are an artist.

—St. Francis of Assisi

In this book, I talk a lot about the hands and the head of learning, but the core of what this book is about is the artistry we need to create in our students, and that will only come if we also attend to their hearts and souls.

When you talk about these issues in school, people tend to get nervous. The imperative of separation of church and state makes it very difficult to discuss the issue of "soul," and if you talk about "heart," you are seen as soft and squishy. Yet there is nothing in life that is not affected at its core by these two elements. This is most especially true of education. As I have repeated throughout this book, the issue of making schools meaningful and engaging is core to the kind of transformation I think we need. The issues of intrinsic motivation, of connection, of collaborative behavior, and of caring all grow from the soil of the heart and soul.

The issue of spirituality has been emerging in our society, not the least of which is spirituality in education. This has been a particular interest of mine for some time. I coauthored a book, *The Spiritual Dimension of Leadership*, with Steven Sokolow (Houston & Sokolow, 2006) that delved into this topic. I serve as president of the Center for Empowered Leadership, which is based on a number of spiritual principles, so I have thought a lot about this topic. Others have written eloquently on the spiritual life of children. It is not my intent to try to explore this topic here because it would require too much time and space. It is my intent to make it clear that we cannot talk about transforming schools if we are not willing to tackle this topic.

There is a big difference between the issue of religion and that of spirituality. It is as great as the difference of pipes and what flows through pipes. There are many different kinds of pipes—copper, lead, or plastic. Different religions tend to be shaped by beliefs and dogmas, and if you join a church, you are expected to accept its teachings—you have to accept their "pipe." Spirituality is that which is common to all of us—it is the water flowing through the pipes. It is something all humans share even though it goes by many different names. It is the sense we are all connected, that we have a need to connect to our deepest selves, and that we tend to connect to something greater than ourselves. It is an attempt to grapple with that part of us known as the soul—that part that makes us more than a sack of meat and bones.

Likewise, the key difference between the work of education and other industries is that our production and our products are human—those entities with a soul. One might argue this is also true of medicine, but the massive intrusion of technology and drugs make medicine a bit less human than it once was. Education, at its core, remains a human enterprise. The work of delivering education is still carried out by teachers. As I argue in this book, we need to embrace technology, but at this point, our technology is largely human. And although we are supposed to produce a product and much of the current angst around education is in the perception, we are failing at that: The "product" we are dealing with is human.

This is why comparisons with business will always be a little invidious and lame. Every child comes to us unique, with different strengths, needs, gifts, and issues. And their teacher is supposed to deliver learning to them. Yet the learning has to be created internally if we want anything more than rote recitation. So we have to appeal to all those things that are on the inside. Throughout this book, I have used the word "caring" and even deigned to use the *L* word—love—on several occasions. The reality is that the learning experience is an emotional experience. We learn from brain research that the primitive brain sets many of the conditions for learning, and those are driven by emotion. Our response to teachers such as Mrs. Spurlock and Mrs. Sang are largely responses of the heart. So *feeling* and *emotion* and *heart* are at the center of what we do.

Writer Terry Deal (Deal & Deal Redman, 2008) has stated, "Schools are out of whack because their soul has shriveled and their spirit has dampened, not simply because they lack rigorous standards or tangible results." The irony is that the more schools push simply toward rigorous standards and tangible results, the more shriveling and dampening we'll see. In many ways, this is simply an issue of what is inside and what is outside. The more schools push and are pushed through external pressure, the more difficult it will be for the souls to soar and the hearts to sing. Heart and soul is an inside job, but they can easily be adversely affected from the outside. The best way for the heart and soul to thrive is to be greeted in honest connection to other hearts and souls. As I have pointed out, you cannot bludgeon people to greatness. You cannot coerce and intimidate your way to excellence. These products must come from within and must be given, not taken.

This is why the words such as "connection," "compassion," and "caring" are so important to the process of learning. When they are present, they release the inside of the children so that they can grow and learn. When they are absent, then learning is being done in a barren and arid place, and nothing will grow there.

For education to become something that it is not, and there is general agreement by everyone that is needed, then it can only happen when relationships are nurtured, needs are supported, and cooperation and collaboration are the coin of the realm. It is not enough not to inflict pain on others or even to feel their pain. We have to know what it means to them and how it affects them. This is a heart and soul connection.

In a graduation speech to a medical school, actor Alan Alda (2007), who was best known for playing a surgeon on television, gave these medical school graduates advice that should be on the wall of every classroom in America. He told them, "The heart bone is connected to the head bone. Don't let them come apart." What Alda was saying is that the way to a people's brains is through their hearts. That is true for medicine, and it is central to education. The head and the heart are inextricably connected, and if we try to separate them, both will suffer or shrivel, as Deal (Deal & Deal Redman, 2008) suggests.

So we must know more about how the head works and apply solutions to that need. We must know more about the "how's" and "what's" of learning. We must attend to our structures, methods, and processes. But at the center of the work of education is a true connection to what is core to our children—how they feel and what they value and what makes their souls sing. We must be clear about what is most important, and it isn't tests and standards. It is the hearts and souls of our children—for they are the heart and soul of our future.

CHAPTER EIGHTEEN

A School Worthy of Our Children—A Fable

The future belongs to those who believe in the beauty of their dreams.

—Eleanor Roosevelt

Worthy Elementary School doesn't really look like a very worthy school at all. In fact, it doesn't even look like that much like a school. Several of us had been invited to visit because it was doing education very differently than we were accustomed. We wanted to see what a school worthy of children might look like. Worthy sits in a renovated warehouse with a large vacant lot next to it, which resembles a playground, a bit. There is a modified obstacle course on the playground; a garden sits in one corner, and a big dig area in another. A few students are digging in the ground as we pull into the parking lot. A few others are working in the garden, and a group is going through the challenge course. We walk over to the first group to discover they are digging for artifacts that had been buried there by a couple of archeologists from the nearby university. One of the archeologist volunteers is helping them. They are learning how real archeologists do their

work. Some of the kids have unearthed pottery shards and are discussing with the archeologist what age they may be from and
what exactly they may have originally been. This leads to a rich
discussion on what kind of culture created these items and what
life might have been like for those who made the artifacts. He
turns their questions back on them and tells them how they might
research to get the answers to their questions. We stroll over to the
garden, and the students are so engrossed in their work they don't
even look up and note our arrival. They are tending a number of
vegetable plants, some flowers, and a few plants that aren't recog-
nizable. Finally, a young man about 10 years old notices our
arrival. He smiles and starts to tell us that the strange plants are
some that they have been trying to develop to see if they can blend
some of the vegetables to make them hardier. He explains they are
studying genetic engineering and are trying out some of their
ideas. He seems genuinely excited about the whole thing and
quickly returns to his work.

As we enter the school, we find a large open space with many
different areas created by bookcases and other artificial walls. We
are surprised to find how few students there are around the great
space. We expected to see more. We have difficulty spotting a
teacher who will tell us what is going on. Finally, a girl, who is
about 13 years old, notices us and gives us a big smile. She leaves
her work, which seems to be some sort of wiring activity, and
strolls over to us and welcomes us to her school. Before we can
ask, she tells us that she is trying to build her own computer. This
is the second one she has done, and it is going to be much more
powerful than her first, and she admits she is struggling a bit
because it much more complex than her first effort. She is working
on the schematics, so she can begin gathering the parts she will
need. She tells us her mentor, who is a student at Worthy High,
which is located nearby, is coming by this afternoon to help her.
She informs us he is a real computer "genius," and she is sure he
will help her finish the project in good fashion. We asked her about
the teachers, and she points to a small group about 20-feet away
that is engrossed in some sort of activity.

We finally spot an adult on the edge of the group, encouraging the students in their work. As the group finishes up, the
teacher comes over to us. She is a young lady, about 22 years old.
She tells us she is a *novice* teacher, and she is a part of the *learning*

team that works with about 125 students. There is another novice on the team, two teachers, and a team leader. She says they also have two part-time paraprofessionals and are getting two student teachers from the university next term. She explains that the "novice" title is conferred on completion of teacher training, and she will serve in this role until she demonstrates enough competence to become a teacher. She says she expects this will take her two or three years if she continues to progress. She explains that the team she works with will determine when she is ready to move up. She went on to explain that the novices work under the direction of the teachers, and the teachers work under the leadership of the team leader. Out of the side of her mouth she whispers that the "team leader" title is a bit of a euphemism because her leader is really a master teacher—one of the best in the school—and she feels very lucky to be working with her. She feels like she is learning as much as the students and that her team leader "rocks." She feels having such a great mentor will speed her movement toward the next step.

We ask her where all the kids are, as there doesn't seem to be 125 in her area. She chuckles and says one group has gone to a museum downtown to study ancient man. She explains they will be taking a number of trips there as they work on their project. This is an outgrowth of a lot of the work in the "shard garden," and one of the university professors is with the group along with one of her colleagues. Another group is out interviewing elderly people about their childhood for their anthropology and American history studies. Still others are being "homeschooled." We are surprised. Homeschooled? How is this possible? She chuckles and explains it isn't like the homeschooling that we know. It just means that the kids are home, working on their computers on projects that require intensive private time, or they may just be practicing. She sees our blank stares and goes on to explain that most of the skills work at Worthy is handled by computers, and the work done in school is group work and directed projects. The work done on the home computers is reviewed by the teachers, and if someone seems stuck, they get some individual tutorial help.

At school, kids are learning how to cooperate and work in teams, and they are also working on their individual projects. Each year, the students identify a major project to work on. For some, like the girl we had met when we came in the building, the project is very hands on and involves making something significant that will require study, research, and application. For others, it may be an extensive written project about a topic of interest. She laughs and says the younger kids always seem to gravitate toward dinosaurs but that gives the teachers a chance to broaden their understanding of geology, animal behavior, and the like. She tells us her learning community is made of students from about nine years old to about fourteen years old. She says there is another learning community of children from five years old to nine years old that is organized the same way, but of course, their work is less complicated, and they spend more time working with teachers at the school. She excuses herself, as she needs to get to her art group. She tells us they are starting to learn computerized graphic arts, and they need a good deal of support right now.

An older teacher comes over to us. She explains she is the team leader. She apologizes that she doesn't have much time because, in a few minutes, she will be directing about half of the entire group on a discussion of the United States Constitution. She reminds us that an election is coming up in a few months, and it is a great time to study government. She says that, over the next few months, all the kids will get to visit city hall, meet the mayor, and watch the city council at work. She says the kids over at Worthy High get to go to the state capital and will visit with members of the legislature. One kid's project last year involved getting a piece of legislation passed, and even though he has graduated, he is coming back this year to talk to both schools about what he did and why it was important.

We aren't going to get to visit the high school, so we ask her how it differs from the K–8 school we were now in. She explained that if we went to the high school, we would still see small groups working with teachers mastering their advanced subject areas. We would see a lot of computer work being done. Much of the curriculum is done with simulations and gaming. But then she laughed and told us that the school would be pretty quiet and a lot emptier than we might expect. She explained that students only have three years of high school after eighth grade. The first two involve classes, projects, and group activities. It's pretty intense because they have so much to study. In the last year, the students are actually out of the building most of the time working on their senior thesis, which is an individual project that involves their using what they have learned up to this point on a real problem. They come back to the school for seminars and tutorials, but the bulk of their time is spent on their project. I asked her what happens if they goof off and don't get it done. She told me that rarely happens, but when it does, they simply have to keep working until they complete it satisfactorily. Then they get their diploma. She explained that there was no such thing as retention at either school. The work that needed to be completed was pretty clear to everyone, and the students worked as fast or as slow as they needed, but they all ultimately finished the work.

By this time, our heads were spinning because what we were seeing was so different from what we had experienced in school. One of the big takeaways for me was how engaged everyone seemed to be and how happy they appeared. They genuinely seemed to *want* to be there. And everywhere I looked, I noticed how pleasant everyone was to one another. As we left, I was pretty sure that not everything was wonderful there. I suspected, as with any visit, there were problems we didn't see and issues that needed resolution. I was equally sure that Worthy Elementary (and by implication Worthy High) was a lot further down the road toward creating a great learning environment than most of the schools I had attended or visited over my time in education.

And as a former school system leader, I did some math in my head, and it didn't seem to me that what they were doing was very expensive. They paid their teaching staff based on roles. The team leader worked a full year and was paid for the extra time and responsibility of leading the team. The teachers were paid as current teachers are, and the novices where given a beginning salary a bit under current practice. The school obviously invested heavily in technology, and I was certain their transportation costs were significant, as they moved groups around. But so much of what they were doing put the burden of work on the students, which really costs less than trying to supervise them every minute. And they were using the resources of the community to supplement their work.

As we left the building, we noticed many very young children in one area and a number of adults in their vicinity. We asked one of the adults, who seemed to be leaving, what that was about, and he explained it was the day care and preschool program. He also pointed out a room where he said volunteer nurses and doctors screened and gave the young children regular health checkups. Another area next to it was a classroom for parents. It was a friendly place they could come to hone their parenting skills. He told us it was a little slow right now, but would be buzzing later in the day, as parents came home from work and stopped by the school for classes.

We left Worthy feeling like they were really on to something there. I couldn't wait to tell the world about it. And I am. Right here.

Study Guide

Make it so.

—Captain, Jean-Luc Picard, Captain,
USS Enterprise, *Star Trek: The Next Generation*

In this book, I have tried to offer a fair critique of current education and a compelling vision for what it might become—a place where children's dreams are honored and empowered. But I am a strong believer in the power of those nearest the work making this vision real. For this reason, I offer this study guide for teacher preparation classes, faculties, district staff, or parent groups to explore how they might move their school or district toward this possibility. The questions offered are here to serve as a conversation starter or a way planning can be undertaken to make the vision of this book a reality.

CHAPTER ONE

My Wings

1. What are the ways you empower your students or staff to be all they can be?

2. How do you help students take personal responsibility for their learning and success?

3. What would your students or staff tell you about how you nourish and support creativity in them?

4. How do you get students to dream bigger dreams for themselves?

5. What do you think the role of setting expectations is in learning and success?

6. What are the ways you have planted the seeds of possibility in your students this year, this month, this week, and today? What specifically could you do that would redouble your efforts and success with this?

7. What causes you to maintain a never-give-up approach with your students?

8. What do you find yourself saying to students who can't seem to develop an expanded vision for their future?

9. What are the three most successful strategies you have used or observed others using that result in students taking more responsibility for their learning?

10. What would a child experience in a school where educators demonstrated the goal of giving wings to children's dreams? What would it take for you as a teacher or administrator to move your school in that direction?

CHAPTER TWO

Teachers: Magicians and Conductors

1. Try to get a vision of one or two teachers who seemed to have the greatest impact on you as a student. What were their defining characteristics, and how did those things have an impact on your school experience?

2. What factors do you think account for the loss of both experienced and new teachers each year? What does your school system do to support and reward good teachers?

3. What is the artistry of teaching all about?

4. How would you create more magicians and conductors? Do you believe this quality can be "trained" through the usual teacher education programs?

CHAPTER THREE

Attitude = Altitude

1. What's your number one, all-time winner for getting kids to want to learn?

2. How would you figure out what intrinsic conditions (connectors) would cause a child to want to learn?

3. How could you create more powerful connections between students and the curriculum?

4. What is it about being an educator that sometimes makes you reluctant to acknowledge the transformative power of love in the learning process?

5. How could you redesign schools and schooling so that students couldn't wait to get there every day?

CHAPTER FOUR

Leaning Our Ladder Against the Right Wall

1. What types of thinking lead to misdiagnosing issues in American education?

2. Dr. Houston contends that we are making incremental progress in an exponential world. What is different about an exponential world, and what are the implications of that for our practice?

3. How would you characterize the current context for education in America? What do you need to teach students that will enable them to be productive citizens in the 21st century?

4. In what ways could you redesign American education to better fit the current context and expectations?

5. What have been the most successful strategies in American education for helping all students learn regardless of race, gender, or socioeconomic status? What strategies outside of education might you adapt and implement?

CHAPTER FIVE

Crawling Out of the Box

1. If all things were possible and nothing was sacred about our history with American education, identify a set of beliefs and values that you think should become the foundation or philosophy for the redesign of education for the 21st century.

2. Much has been said about the need for schools to produce students who effectively compete in a technology-based, global community in the 21st century. What outcomes, skills, and attitudes would you want your students to demonstrate to be fully able to contribute to such a world?

3. Given your beliefs about 21st-century education and the skills students need to compete, how would you design a school system for our children? What things may need to change in the broader American culture to support such a system and the success of all learners?

CHAPTER SIX

How It Ought to Be

1. What recent or past innovations have you implemented that made a significant and demonstrable difference in student learning or motivation to learn? What was it about those innovations that made such a difference in student learning, and how did you know they did?

2. Develop a set of criteria for accepting or rejecting educational innovations in your school or school system.

3. What do you believe high school education should be about in today's world? We are familiar with challenges to high school reform, but what current opportunities for redesign do you see? What are some important first steps in your school system?

CHAPTER SEVEN

Getting Kids Ready for Democracy

1. In today's context, how do schools continue to serve the noble purpose of creating a public? What challenges exist in the pursuit of this goal? What is it about our current system that enables us to achieve this goal?

2. What examples of healthy conflict resolution do you observe in your school and school system? In what ways do you model this for your students, and what strategies do you use to teach these skills?

3. What are the ways you could provide walkabout real-world experiences for your students? How could the concepts of walkabouts and service learning add to the conversation about high school reform?

4. What is your belief about the place of teaching values and character in education today? How do your beliefs about this matter play out in your classroom or school system?

CHAPTER EIGHT

Getting Kids Ready for School—Raising the Village

1. How would a visitor to your school or school system know that children are the central client and focus? What are the ways you could strengthen this even more?

2. How would you use your schools to create a stronger community?

3. Name things about your school or school system that send the message that it is parent and community friendly. In spite of Columbine–like security measures, what do you think parents say about this issue, and how do you know?

4. What do you see in your professional practice that demonstrates healership leadership?

5. How would you use parents to enhance the learning environment for students?

6. What do you believe about the role of schools in parenting training?

7. How can you get the 70% of the community who do not have children in schools to support public education?

8. In your view, should schools be responsible for birth to Grade 12 education? Why, or why not?

CHAPTER NINE

Getting Schools Ready for Kids

1. What seems to sabotage or inhibit real change in your school or district?

2. What are your views about the question, "Is education instrumental or fundamental?" How does your view play out in your educational practice?

3. What could you set as school goals besides raising test scores that, in the end, would raise scores but so much more?

4. What things in your educational practice help students create knowledge rather than simply acquiring it?

5. How have you rigorously self-assessed your teaching or leadership strategies in terms of effect on student learning? What did you learn in that process, and how did it lead to growth for you and students?

6. What about the structure, curriculum, and teaching methods in your school demonstrate that the school fits the students? How could you make it an even better fit?

CHAPTER TEN

Getting the Words and the Symbols Right

1. What messages do we send to students through our language and nonverbal behaviors?

2. What tells you that you are a good listener to students and other adults?

3. How could the educational experience for your students improve if we stopped viewing others through our lens and tried to understand others' perspectives?

4. How can we help technology-dependant students develop powerful interpersonal communication skills?

5. If you agree that writing, speaking, and listening continue to be vital skills needed in the 21st century, how might you redesign curriculum, instruction, and even the school environment to enable the development of these skills?

6. How can you create balance between the need for efficiency and the need for personal communication?

7. It has been said that "education is a people business." Do you continue to believe this, and how has the technology and the communication age had an impact on the people business? What would you gain and what would you lose by rehumanizing communication in your schools?

CHAPTER ELEVEN

Horse Whispering: Harnessing Technology to Enhance Learning

1. What keeps you from fully maximizing the use of technology to support student learning? How could you meet those challenges?

2. What are two or three goals you have for students, and how could technology assist them in achieving those goals?

3. What would you see if your school truly embraced the brave new world of ubiquitous technology in the learning process?

4. In what ways do you use technology to assist in development or implementation of individual learning plans for students?

CHAPTER TWELVE

The Brain Is a Terrible Thing to Waste

1. What are ways you have consciously incorporated research about how the brain learns into practice in the last five years? What is your plan for the next five years? How do you assess the legitimacy and potential usefulness of this research?

2. What tells you that you are a mindful practitioner?

3. Think of examples where research about how the brain learns has become the foundation for instructional practice district wide. What was the process for this innovation? How has the impact on students been assessed? What adjustments have been necessary?

CHAPTER THIRTEEN

Creativity and the Arts: The Surry, Not the Fringe

1. How does a creative person think and approach challenges?

2. What do you see coming in the 21st-century world that will require creative solutions?

3. What skills do you think students will need to learn to be productive and successful in the 21st century? How are your schools gearing up to help students develop these skills?

4. Specifically, how do you support creativity and imagination in your students? How will you teach students to create unique solutions to existing or future problems?

5. What things have you always assumed to be true about educating students that likely will not be true in the 21st century?

CHAPTER FOURTEEN

Authentic Accountability

1. Pretend you have the power to design an accountability system for your school or school system. (Too bad we have

to pretend!) What guiding assumptions underlie your plan? What are the actionable pieces of the plan? How could you implement this system alongside No Child Left Behind requirements?

2. In what ways would students, parents, educators, and your community benefit from your plan?

CHAPTER FIFTEEN

Lead Is Not a Four-Letter Word

1. What are the leadership challenges facing school leaders in the 21st century?

2. Given those challenges, in what ways do you believe leaders must behave differently than ever before?

3. What assumptions, values, or beliefs underlie your 21st-century leadership model?

4. What is your plan for transformation and change over the next five years?

CHAPTER SIXTEEN

Bored of Education

1. If governance by the board and superintendent team in your district truly focused on giving wings to children's dreams, what aspects of governance would be transformed, and how might that happen?

2. What common interests currently exist between the board of education, the superintendent, and the teacher's union regarding governance of the school system? How might those common interests be used as a basis for positive change in the district?

3. Develop a vision for 21st-century school governance. What assumptions would you build into this model? What would its components look like? How would the model address the needs of schools and students in the 21st century?

CHAPTER SEVENTEEN

Dealing With the Heart and Soul

1. Regardless of your role in the school district, what five things could you do this week or month to bring greater heart and soul into your work with students?

2. How do you imagine this approach might impact students?

3. In what ways might it change you?

CHAPTER EIGHTEEN

A School Worthy of Our Children—A Fable

1. In your view, what are the key characteristics of a school worthy of our children?

2. What steps can you take to transform your school this month, this year, and in the next five years?

3. What will the challenges be? What things will support your plan for transformation?

4. How will your students benefit from the transformation of their school?

5. How will you know your plan is benefiting students?

References

Alda, A. (2007). *Things I overheard while talking to myself.* New York: Random House.

Carson, C. C., Huelskamp, R. M., & Woodall, T. D. (1991). *Perspectives on education in America.* Albuquerque, NM: Systems Studies Department, Sandia National Laboratories.

Character Counts. (2010). The six pillars of character. *Josephson Institute.* Retrieved from http://charactercounts.org/sixpillars.html.

Chopra, D. (2002, September). The soul of leadership: By looking inward, any individual has the capacity to rise to greatness. *School Administrator, 59*(8), 10–12.

Christensen, C., Horn, M. B., & Johnson, C. W. (2008). *Disrupting class: How disruptive innovation will change the way the world learns.* New York: McGraw-Hill.

Condry, J., & Chambers, J. (1978). Intrinsic motivation and the process of learning. In M. R Lepper & D. Greene (Eds,), *The hidden costs of reward.* Hillldale, New Jersey: Lawrence Erlbaum.

Cooper, H., Nye, B., Charlton, K., Lindsay, J., & Greathouse, S. (1996).The effects of summer vacation on achievement test scores: A narrative and meta-analytic review. *Review of Educational Research, 66*(3), 207–266.

Deal, T. E., & Deal Redman, P. (2008), Reviving the soul of teaching: Balancing metrics and magic. Thousand Oaks, CA: Corwin.

Doidge, N. (2007). *The brain that changes itself.* New York. Penguin Books.

Dyer, W. (2004). *The power of intention: Learning to co-create your world your way.* Carlsbad, California: Hay House.

Farson, R. (1997). *Management of the absurd: The paradoxes of leadership.* New York: Touchstone.

Florida, R. (2002). *The rise of the creative class and how it is transforming work, leisure, community and everyday living.* New York: Basic Books.

Frankenberg, E., Siegel-Hawley, G., & Wang, J. (2010). *Choice without equity: Charter school segregation and the need for civil rights standards.* Retrieved from http://www.civilrightsproject.ucla.edu/news/press releases/CRP-Choices-Without-Equity-report.pdf.

Friedman, T. (2005). *The earth is flat: A brief history of the 21st century.* New York: Farrar, Strauss and Giroux.

Gibbons, M. (1974). Walkabout: Searching for the right passage from childhood and school. *Phi Delta Kappan, 55*(9), 596–602.

Harris, P. & Smith, B. (2010, May 12). An idea to consider: The purpose is the point. *Education Week, 29*, p. 32.

Hart, B., & Risley, T. (2003). The early catastrophe: The 30 million word gap by age 3. *American Educator, 27*(1). Retrieved from http://archive.aft.org/pubs-reports/american_educator/spring2003/catastrophe.html.

Houston, P., & Sokolow, S. (2006). *The spiritual dimension of leadership.* Thousand Oaks, CA: Corwin.

Jazzy Jeff & Fresh Prince. (1998). Parents just don't understand. On *Greatest Hits.* [CD]. New York: Jive.

Kozol, J. (1991). *Savage inequalities: Children in America's schools.* New York: Crown.

Kozol, J. (1995). *Amazing grace.* New York: Crown.

Langer, E. (1989). *Mindfulness.* Cambridge, MA: Da Capo Press.

Marshall, H. H. (1987, November). Motivational strategies of three fifth-grade teachers. *Elementary School Journal, 88*(2), 135–150.

National Commission on Excellence in Education. (1983). *A nation at risk: The imperative for education reform: An open letter to the American people.* Retrieved from http://datacenter.spps.org/sites/2259653e-ffb3-45ba-8fd6-04a024ecf7a4/uploads/SOTW_A_Nation_at_Risk_1983.pdf.

National Commission on Terrorist Attacks upon the United States (2004). *The 9/11 Commission Report.* New York: W. W. Norton & Company.

Nichols, S. L., & Berliner, D. (2007). Collateral damage: How high stakes testing corrupts America's schools. Cambridge, MA: Harvard Press.

Pink, D. (2005). *A whole new mind: Moving from the Information Age to the Conceptual Age.* New York: Riverhead Books.

Pink, D. (2009). *Drive: The surprising truth about what motivates us.* New York: Riverhead Books.

Ramo, J. C. (2009). *The age of the unthinkable.* New York: Little, Brown & Company.

Roberts, M. (1996). *The man who listens to horses: The story of a real-life horse whisperer.* New York: Random House.

Robinson, S. K. (2001). *Out of our minds: Learning to be creative.* Chichester, England: Capstone.

Schweinhart, L. J. (1994). *The lasting benefits of preschool programs.* Urbana, IL: ERIC Clearinghouse on Elementary and Early Childhood Education. (ERIC Identifier: ED365478)

Williams, J. P., & Blomquist, A. C. (Producers). (2003). *Blue collar comedy tour.* [DVD]. Bill Engvall. United States: Parallel Entertainment.

Wolfe, P. (2003). Brain research and education: Fad or foundation. *Mind Matters.* Retrieved from http://www.patwolfe.com/index.php?pid=100.

Zakaria, F. (2008). *The Post-American world.* New York W. W. Norton.

CORWIN
A SAGE Company

The Corwin logo—a raven striding across an open book—represents the union of courage and learning. Corwin is committed to improving education for all learners by publishing books and other professional development resources for those serving the field of PreK–12 education. By providing practical, hands-on materials, Corwin continues to carry out the promise of its motto: **"Helping Educators Do Their Work Better."**

AMERICAN ASSOCIATION
OF SCHOOL ADMINISTRATORS

The American Association of School Administrators, founded in 1865, is the professional organization for more than 13,000 educational leaders across the United States. AASA's mission is to support and develop effective school system leaders who are dedicated to the highest quality public education for all children. For more information, visit www.aasa.org.